MYSELF AND OTHERS

*A Study in Our Knowledge
of Minds*

MYSELF AND OTHERS

A Study in Our Knowledge of Minds

———◆———

DON LOCKE

OXFORD
AT THE CLARENDON PRESS
1968

Oxford University Press, Ely House, London W. 1

GLASGOW NEW YORK TORONTO MELBOURNE WELLINGTON
CAPE TOWN SALISBURY IBADAN NAIROBI LUSAKA ADDIS ABABA
BOMBAY CALCUTTA MADRAS KARACHI LAHORE DACCA
KUALA LUMPUR HONG KONG TOKYO

PRINTED IN GRE   BRITAIN

CONTENTS

ACKNOWLEDGEMENTS

THIS study is really a case of diminished plagiarism—diminished because I refuse to draw the usual conclusions from points I steal from others—and it will be obvious that I have borrowed most from those I attack most. I would like to thank the University of Newcastle upon Tyne for a period of study leave which enabled me to bring this into its final shape; and also the staff and students in the Philosophy Department of the University of Auckland who made many valuable comments and criticisms. I owe a special debt to Professor Roy Holland, of the University of Leeds, who saved me from several mistakes and misunderstandings. His vehement opposition to what I say in Chapter IV, in particular, forced me to be much clearer than I would otherwise have been.

CHAPTER I

The Source of the Problems

1. THERE are two separate questions which I want to discuss: first the question of what is involved in our knowledge of our own minds, and second the question of what is involved in our knowledge of other minds. These questions arise in connexion with certain special, and I would say central, mental characteristics, those which seem in some way to be private, hidden, internal, incorporeal. For despite Professor Ryle's wholesale attack I think it would generally be admitted that there are some mental phenomena which are 'ghostly' in his sense.[1] However, I will not stop to argue this here, nor to argue another conviction of mine, that all that is ghostly within the sphere of the mental, i.e. 'consciousness' in particular, as opposed to 'mind' in general, can be analysed in terms of such conscious processes as perceiving, thinking, in one sense of that word, and imaging or having mental images. Rather I will take perceiving and thinking, in particular, to be paradigm examples of conscious processes, and I will try to show both why such processes might well be described as ghostly, and how it is that certain distinctive problems arise about our knowledge of such processes. Of course 'thinking' and 'thought' can refer to things other than this conscious process, the process which

[1] See, for example, the first part of Jerome Shaffer's excellent summary, 'Recent Work in the Mind–Body Problem', *American Philosophical Quarterly*, 1965.

Plato described as the soul's conversing with itself. We can speak of thinking that the earth is flat or thinking about what you are doing. But when I speak of the conscious process of thinking it is thinking to yourself, thinking 'in your head' —and perhaps this itself covers more than one thing—that I mean. As well as speaking of conscious processes I will also speak of conscious states. These can be thought of as stages, episodes, moments in the history of a conscious process.

My argument is, then, that it is because thinking and perceiving are hidden, silent, internal, incorporeal, ghostly in the sense to be explained, that we have the familiar problems about our knowledge of minds: the problem of our privileged self-knowledge, and the problem of our knowledge of other minds. This means that these problems arise only in relation to such conscious processes, and not in relation to other mental attributes, such as knowledge, memory, intentions, moods, or character traits, except in so far as they happen to involve perceiving and thinking. But let us begin by asking in what sense perceiving and thinking can be said to be ghostly, hidden, incorporeal.

It seems that to say that perceiving, for example, is incorporeal might mean any or all of three things: it might mean that it is not solid, not even in the way in which butter, balloons, and thin ice are solid; it might mean that it has no physical location; or it might mean that it cannot be perceived. Yet it would be ridiculous to insist that perceiving is not solid, for perceiving is a process, and what processes are solid? Are running, breathing, saluting solid? The point should rather be that perceiving does not consist in changes or movements of things which are solid, in the way that running consists in various movements of legs, breathing in movements of lungs, and saluting in movements of hands. Similarly with the suggestion that perceiving has no physical location. The point cannot be that it does not go on anywhere, for clearly perceiving goes on in the street and on the parade ground just as much as running, breathing, and saluting do. The point must rather be that perceiving does not consist in changes or movements of things which have a spatial location, things like legs, lungs, and hands. Finally, to say that perceiving cannot be perceived seems to mean that it does not consist in changes or movements of perceptible items, things which we can perceive as we perceive legs, lungs, and hands.

It might be said that perceiving and thinking do consist in changes in solid, or partially solid, locatable, and perceptible items, viz. brain cells. Nevertheless those who hold that perceiving and thinking are, in fact, identical with the workings of, the goings-on in, various parts of the brain and the nervous system, allow that this is not a necessary identity. They agree that 'I see a hippopotamus' does not mean, even in part, that certain cells in the optic centres of the brain are being activated, even though it may be true that seeing a hippopotamus is, in fact, identical with having those brain cells activated.[1] But on the other hand, 'I am running' does mean, at least in part, that my legs are moving in certain ways, and 'I am breathing' does mean, at least in part, that my lungs are moving in a certain way. So the fact remains that perceiving does not consist in changes in brain cells in the way that running consists, at least in part, in movements

[1] Cf. J. J. C. Smart, *Philosophy and Scientific Realism* (Routledge & Kegan Paul), p. 92.

of the legs, and breathing consists, at least in part, in movements of the lungs.

So it is because perceiving and thinking are processes
which do not consist in, or we might prefer to say do not
necessarily involve, changes or movements in particular
solid, locatable, perceptible items, that we think of them as
ghostly or incorporeal processes. Even the 'process' of rising
in a crescendo, which does not consist in changes of solid or
strictly locatable items, is not thought of as ghostly in the
way that thinking and perceiving are, because it does at
least consist in changes in perceptible items, sounds, which
are to be heard in certain places. This also explains why we
think of perceiving and thinking as mental, as occurring 'in
the mind', in a way that answering a question or playing a
trick on a friend—both of which are things which only a
conscious being, a being with a mind, could do—are not.
The contrast between the mental and the physical is to a
considerable extent the contrast between things which have
a perceptible spatio-temporal location and things which do
not. Finally the fact that perceiving and thinking do not consist in changes of solid, locatable, perceptible items also
explains why we think of them as hidden, silent, and internal. If we cannot bump into, come across, perceive, these
processes going on, how can we know that they are going
on? They must be hidden from us, concealed within a person's mind (wherever that is), discoverable only by the
person whose mind, whose thinking and perceiving, it is.

This is the source of our problems about the knowledge of
minds. I can know that I or another person is breathing by
feeling the lungs move, hearing the breath, and so on. But
if nothing can be felt, heard, or seen which would count as

feeling, hearing, or seeing the thinking or perceiving, how can I know that anyone is thinking or perceiving, or what thinking and perceiving are like? Thus there is a problem about our knowledge of minds inasmuch as minds, consciousnesses, or at any rate conscious processes are, in the sense explained, 'ghostly'.

2. There is also a further problem inasmuch as these conscious processes are also 'private'. This again is something that has to be explained.

When we say that something—a house, a hiccup, a pain, or a thought—is private there are four things that might be meant; we can distinguish at least four types of privacy:[1]

(1) Privacy of ownership ('o-private'). A thing is 'o-private' if it is owned by or belongs to a particular person or group of persons; it is in this sense that my dog, my house, and my typewriter are all private. Notice that this does not mean that others cannot come to own these things, nor that I cannot share them with others, although then, of course, they would cease to be mine or mine alone. Nor does it mean that others cannot perceive them.

(2) Logical privacy ('l-private'). A thing is 'l-private' if it cannot, logically cannot, be owned by or shared with others. It is logically possible that the dog, house, or typewriter that I now own should be owned by someone else; the transfer of ownership would not mean that they must be numerically different things. But it is not logically possible for others to have my hiccups or my voice, or to perform my actions. Nor can Poland have Bulgaria's history,

---

[1] What follows is taken, with several changes, from my 'The Privacy of Pains', *Analysis*, 1964.

although, *pace* Ryle (*Concept of Mind*, Hutchinsons, p. 209), Venus might, in some cosmological upheaval, come to have Neptune's satellites. Others cannot own *this* hiccup, *this* voice, or *this* action, for then it would not be this hiccup, voice, or action, but some other, numerically different, one. The point is that hiccups, voices, and actions are individuated by reference to the person who owns them, so that what makes this voice the voice that it is is the fact that it belongs to this person, whereas the fact that this house is owned by me is quite accidental to its being this particular house.

(3) Mental privacy ('m-private'). A thing is 'm-private' if only one person can perceive it. After-images and hallucinations, but not dogs or hiccups, are normally private in this sense. You can see my dog, hear—even feel—my hiccups, but you cannot see my after-images or hear the buzzing in my ears.

(4) Epistemological privacy ('e-private'). A thing is 'e-private' if only one person can know about it. But although there may be facts which only the one person does know —Peg Leg Pete may be the only one who knows where the treasure is buried—it is arguable that there can be nothing which is private in this sense, which only one person *can* know. What is true is that there are some things—a man's intentions are an example—which only one person can know of *in the way that he does*. To use another technical term: I have 'privileged access' to my intentions, I do not have to discover what they are in the way that others do. It is a considerable jump from saying this to saying that others cannot know about my intentions at all, a jump which requires the quite fantastic premiss that there is and can be only one way of knowing an intention, viz. forming it

yourself. Since this premiss is clearly unacceptable I will talk about privileged access rather than about epistemological privacy. It is obvious that in at least some cases we do not have to learn about our intentions in the way that others do, but it is far from obvious that others cannot learn of our intentions at all.

In which of these senses, then, are such conscious processes as thinking and perceiving private? First of all, they are not only o-private but also l-private, inasmuch as all processes are individuated by reference to the thing or person to whom that process 'belongs'. In this their privacy does not differ from that of running, breathing, or saluting. Moreover they are not, and cannot be, m-private, for the simple reason that my perceiving (as opposed to what I perceive) and my thinking are not perceptible at all, not even by me. But most important of all, although perceiving and thinking are not e-private, we do have privileged access to them. Others do not know that or what I am thinking or perceiving in the way that I know it; I do not, as others do, have to find out whether or what I am perceiving or thinking. This means that there is an important difference between our knowledge of our own minds and our knowledge of other minds, and as well as explaining how we can know about thinking and perceiving at all, we will also have to explain this difference. That is, we will have to consider first what the nature of our privileged access to our perceiving and thinking is, and second what the consequences are of this fact that we cannot know other people's minds in the way that they know them. But before going on to these questions I want to say something about our knowledge of pains and other bodily sensations.

3. It is rather surprising—surprising because pains are usually thought of as *bodily* sensations—that when contemporary philosophers discuss such topics as introspection or the other minds problem they typically fix on pains as their prime example. In fact the problems about knowledge of pains— my own and other people's—are very different from the problems about knowledge of the things 'in' my own and other people's minds. For a start pains are not 'in' minds at all; they are in teeth, toes, and necks. However, the crucial difference between bodily sensations and such things as perceiving and thinking is that bodily sensations can be perceived, felt, whereas perceiving and thinking cannot (this seems to me a truth of logic). There are epistemological problems about bodily sensations because they are m-private, because only the one person can feel them; there are epistemological problems about conscious processes because they cannot be perceived at all.

Pains, like conscious processes, are l-private. You cannot own my pain any more than you can think my thoughts, breathe my sighs, or have my voice; others cannot own *this* pain, for then it would not be this pain but some other, numerically different, one. Professor R. D. Bradley has suggested to me a case where we might want to say that the same pain is now located in a different body. Suppose that a faith-healer runs his hands along Smith's arthritic limbs, so that the pain passes into the faith-healer's hands, to be washed away in running water. It is hard to know how to describe this possibility, but it seems to me that even if we did say that Smith's pain is now located and felt in the faith-healer's hands, we would still be saying that it is *Smith's* pain and not the faith-healer's. If the pain is still the same pain then it is still Smith's pain, even though Smith no longer feels it. This may sound odd, but anything we say in such a case is bound to sound odd. Moreover, it will sound less odd once we realize that there is a difference between owning a pain and feeling it.

Ryle (*Concept of Mind*, p. 209) says, 'Just as you cannot, in logic, hold my catches, win my races, eat my meals, frown my frowns or dream my dreams, so you cannot have my twinges or after-images.' This is true only if 'have' here means 'own', for the fact that you cannot own my twinges or after-images does not mean that you cannot feel or see them, any more than the fact that you cannot frown my frowns means that you cannot feel or see my frowns. The mental privacy of twinges, tickles, and pains is a contingent, not a necessary, fact; the idea that it is logically impossible for one person to feel another's pains is due largely to the failure to distinguish what I am calling 'logical privacy' from what I am calling 'mental privacy'. It may be a logical impossibility for others to own my pains, but there are possible circumstances in which we would talk of feeling one another's pains, twinges, and tickles.

For example, it is only a contingent fact that our nervous systems are not connected in such a way that whenever you have a toothache I can feel it, not in my tooth but in yours. It might be objected that if everyone felt everything that everyone else did, this would simply break down the distinction between one person and another, so that instead of talking about different people feeling the same pain we should rather talk about one person with one complex body. But even if this is so, which I doubt, we do not need to suppose that all pains are felt by everybody, but only that it is possible to feel another's pains if we wish to. We might, for example, think of ourselves as being able to 'plug into' another's nervous system in order to feel his pain. 'How unpleasant', we say, and hastily unplug again. Plugging into another in order to feel his pain would be like opening your eyes in order to see what is in front of you, putting the sauce on your tongue in order to taste it, or putting your nose near the rose in order to smell it.[1]

Pains and other bodily sensations, then, are m-private, and this is how we come to have privileged access to them. You can, of course, know that I have a pain, but I do not have to find this out in the way that you do, if only because I do not have to find this out at all. Nevertheless the mental privacy of pains is only a contingent matter, dependent upon certain facts about our nervous system. If things were such that others could feel my pains then I would no longer have this privileged access. No doubt I would still be in the best position to know, but my knowledge that there is a pain in my tooth would no more be privileged than my knowledge that I am now writing these words. This means that our privileged access to the existence and nature of our bodily sensations is quite different from our privileged access to our thinking and perceiving, or for that matter to our perceiving, our awareness, of our bodily sensations. We have privileged access to our pains because they are m-private, because only I can feel my pains, whereas conscious processes cannot be felt or perceived at all, by anyone.

Bodily sensations and conscious processes are usually treated together because ordinarily we do not distinguish

[1] This possibility and its consequences are discussed more fully in my 'The Privacy of Pains', *Analysis*, 1964.

between 'There is a pain in my tooth', 'I have a pain in my tooth', and 'I feel a pain in my tooth'. We could distinguish them and, if things were different, if we could feel other people's pains, we would distinguish them, but as things are we do not. Nevertheless there is a definite difference between 'How do I know that there is a pain in my tooth?' and 'How do I know that I feel a pain in my tooth?' I know that there *is* a pain in my tooth because I feel it there, just as I know there is a book on my desk because I see it there. The only differences are that I always notice the pains in my teeth, and I am the only one who can notice them, whereas I do not always notice books on desks, and other people can notice them as well as I. But on the other hand I do not know that I *feel* a pain in my tooth in anything like the way that I know there is a book on the desk. I feel the pain, certainly, and that is why I know that I do, but I do not perceive or feel the feeling of the pain any more than I perceive or see the seeing of the book. True, we often speak of pains as 'feelings of pain'; my point is not that we cannot perceive or feel such 'feelings of pain' but that we cannot perceive or feel perceivings of pain.

So if we are to avoid confusion we had best state our problems not in terms of knowing that there *is* a pain in someone's tooth, but in terms of knowing that he *feels* a pain in his tooth, even though in practice the two go together. For feeling, being aware of, a pain is a conscious state in a way that the pain itself, the bodily sensation, is not; the pain, the sensation, has a location but my feeling, my perceiving, it does not. So when I discuss the other minds problem I will state it not in terms of knowing that another has a pain, but in terms of knowing that he feels it. Similarly the question which concerns us now is not 'How do I know that there is a pain in my tooth?' (answer: because I feel it), but 'How do I know that I feel a pain in my tooth?' This latter is precisely on a par with the questions I now go on to discuss, 'How do I know that I see a rabbit?' and 'How do I know that I am thinking about a rabbit?'

CHAPTER II

Our Knowledge of Our Own Minds

1. OUR question is 'How do I know what is going on in my mind?' Or, more specifically, 'How do I know that I am thinking, perceiving, having an image, etc.?' It might be said that as well as the question 'How do I know *that* I am thinking or perceiving?' there is also the question 'How do I know *what* I am thinking or perceiving?' But it seems to me that in so far as this second question is a question about one's mind or consciousness at all it is covered by the first question. 'How do I know that I am perceiving a rabbit?' is, in effect, ambiguous. I might be asking 'How do I know that the thing I perceive is a rabbit?', in which case I am asking about the object I perceive, not about 'what is going on in my mind'. Or I might be asking 'How do I know that the rabbit, or whatever it is, is perceived by me?', in which case I am asking 'How do I know that I am perceiving whatever it is?' Similarly with thinking, although what corresponds to 'How do I know what I am perceiving?' is not 'How do I know what I am thinking?' but 'How do I know what I am thinking about?'. The thought, what I think, is identical with my thinking it in a way that what is perceived is not identical with my perceiving it. So to know that I am thinking is also to know what I am thinking, and the questions 'How do I know that I am thinking?' and 'How do I know what I am thinking?' are the same. Where there is a difference is between what I am thinking, my thoughts, and

what I am thinking about. And the question 'How do I know that I am thinking about a rabbit?' is, like 'How do I know that I am perceiving a rabbit?', ambiguous. I might be asking 'How do I know that the thing I am thinking about is a rabbit?', in which case I am asking about the object, not about 'what is going on in my mind'. Or I might be asking 'How do I know that I am thinking about it, whatever it is?', in which case I am asking 'How do I know that I am thinking what I am?'

The question is, then: How do I know that I am, for example, thinking, perceiving, feeling a pain? The obvious answer seems to be that I know this just because I am thinking, perceiving, feeling a pain, but this answer, like the question itself, can be misleading. For my thinking or perceiving does not tell me that I am thinking or perceiving in the way that my hearing tells me that there is a train coming. Rather, nothing tells me that I am thinking or perceiving. I just am, and if I am I know that I am. In order to know *what* I am perceiving I may have to look and recognize, but to know *that* I am perceiving all I need do is perceive. In fact it seems that a person couldn't be said to be perceiving, at least not in any straightforward sense, unless he knew that he was.

Indeed this seems to me to be what is meant by calling perception a *conscious* process. It would be a mistake to think that 'conscious' and its variants are essentially connected with mental phenomena, e.g. 'I hit him on the nose quite consciously'. What this means is that it wasn't an accident or a mistake, I knew what I was doing; if I didn't know I was doing it then it wouldn't be a conscious action. So a necessary condition of some item's being a conscious x is that the person to whom it is ascribed knows that it exists or occurs. And that is why conscious processes like thinking and perceiving are said to be private, in the rather misleading sense that our knowledge of them is privileged. Unlike other people I don't have to find out that I am thinking or perceiving; I cannot think or perceive without knowing that I do for the simple reason that, as conscious processes, it follows logically from the fact that they occur that I know that they do. Or, to put it the other way around, they are not said to occur unless I know that they do.

However, this is true only so long as 'perceive' is used in its ordinary, most straightforward, sense. For although perception is naturally thought of as a conscious process there are circumstances in which we want to talk of unconscious, or 'subliminal', perception, and also of unconscious thought. A man may not be aware that something has been quickly flashed in front of him, and yet his subsequent behaviour will suggest that he did, in some sense, perceive it. The message 'X is the best actor' flashed on to a cinema screen has been found to influence the choice of best actor by subjects who did not consciously notice the message, although those who expected the message had no difficulty in perceiving it. Or a man may go to bed worried by a problem and wake up with the correct answer clear in his mind. In such cases it seems correct and appropriate to talk of unconscious perception and unconscious thought. These processes, if such they are, seem to deserve the label 'mental' as much as their conscious equivalents. They raise a definite problem.

The problem is whether unconscious perceiving and thinking are just perceiving and thinking which, unlike most, happen to be unconscious, or whether they are no more perceiving and thinking than a decoy duck is a duck or a would-be judge a judge. Consider the difference between a conscious and an unconscious movement of the hand. The difference between these lies not in what goes on, not in what the hand does, but in my knowledge of what is going on; a conscious movement is the same as an unconscious one, except that the agent knows that he is moving. And so we get the question: how do I know that I move my hand? Is it because I see or feel it moving, or is it because I intend, and of course know that I intend, to move it, or what? Now if conscious perception were, in the same way, simply perception which I happen to know is occurring, we would have the question: how do I know that I am perceiving? The answer 'Because I am' should be no more satisfactory that it is as an answer to the question 'How do I know that I am moving my hand?'—as if, what is obviously false, I could not move without knowing that I do.

The oddity of this question 'How do I know that I am perceiving?' once 'Because I am' is no longer accepted as an answer leads me to say that perception is *essentially* a conscious process. For 'Perception is a conscious process' has the air of a necessary truth, after the pattern of 'Horses are animals', and the very fact that we refer to perceiving and thinking as 'conscious processes' is itself significant. Movements can be conscious, but we do not refer to them as conscious processes. Now if perceiving and thinking are essentially, necessarily, conscious processes, then unconscious perception and unconscious thought are not cases of ordinary perception or thought whose occurrence we happen not to know of. Rather unconscious perception is a degenerate form of perception, so degenerate as not to count as perception, *tout court*, at all, just as a decoy duck is not a genuine kind of duck. Nevertheless the obvious similarities between genuine perception and thought and their unconscious counterparts are sufficient to warrant the borrowing of the words.

Let us agree, then, that thinking and perceiving are essentially conscious processes, which means that they cannot be said to occur unless the person to whom they are ascribed knows that they occur. This raises two questions: Why should this be so? and What is it that occurs, and is known to occur, in the first place? Conscious processes differ from most other processes in that they cannot be perceived, not merely because we lack the necessary equipment, but because they are processes which do not consist in changes or movements of perceptible items. If we could perceive perceiving or thinking then we could talk of them as occurring unperceived, and of our knowing that they were occurring because we happened to perceive them going on, and so of our not knowing that they were occurring because, for some reason, we failed to notice them going on. But since we cannot perceive perceiving or thinking, and so cannot fail to perceive them, we allow that they occur only when we know that they do. That is, the thought of a completely unknowable or completely undetectable process is a little odd, so we regard our knowledge of the occurrence of perception or thought as a necessary condition for the occurrence of those processes. Whether we want to call subliminal perception or unconscious thinking processes I am not at all sure. Personally I would be unhappy about talking of them as 'going on' unless, perhaps, we were to equate them with what goes on in the brain, in which case they would consist in changes and movements of perceptible, solid, and located items.

But we have still not said what kind of an occurrence perceiving and thinking are. They are special, perhaps strange, in that they do not consist in changes or movements of perceptible or located items. Do they then consist in changes or movements of non-perceptible non-located items, items in that special second-status world of the mind whose existence Ryle is so keen to deny? Here surely Ryle is right: the point is not that conscious processes are special and strange in that they consist in changes or movements of special and strange items, but that they are special, perhaps even strange, in that they do not consist in changes or movements of items at all. We might want to ask: how can something occur without some thing moving or changing? If this 'can' is empirical then I would want to agree that this cannot happen, that even perceiving and thinking must involve physical goings-on, goings-on in the brain and elsewhere. But if the question is to be to the point the 'can' must be that of logical possibility. So the assumption behind the question is that all processes must consist in change or movement of more or less concrete, located, or at least perceptible items. The reply must be that this assumption is mistaken, that perceiving and thinking are examples of goings-on which do not consist in such change or movement, and that to fail to appreciate this is to fail, in large part, to appreciate what it is for a being to be conscious in the first place.

However, the main point is that we now have an explanation of our privileged access to such things as thinking and perceiving. They are conscious processes, and at least part of what is meant by calling a process 'conscious' is that the person to whom that process is ascribed knows that it occurs. It is a necessary, analytic, truth that we know of the occurrence of our own conscious processes, that we cannot think or perceive without knowing that we do. My privileged access to my perceiving, thinking, feeling a pain, consists not in any special sensory or intellectual acquaintance with these contents of my consciousness, but in the logical fact that in so far as perceiving, thinking, feeling are conscious processes they cannot occur without my knowing that they do. So the answer to 'How do I know what is going on in my own mind' is, so far as conscious processes and conscious states are concerned, that there is no how, no way or method, at all, and that there is no need of one. The proper question is: Why is there no way of knowing what is going on in one's own mind? Or, if you prefer: Why is our knowledge of our own minds direct or immediate in this way? And the answer is that since these processes which 'go on in our minds' are *conscious* processes they cannot, logically cannot, occur without our knowing that they do.

2. So my answer to the problem of our knowledge of our own minds is that the special knowledge we have here is knowledge of conscious states and processes; that conscious states and processes are, qua conscious, known; and that it is therefore a necessary, analytic, truth that one knows the contents of one's own consciousness. This answer needs some qualification, for conscious processes are not always conscious in this sense. Perception in animals and infants, for example, would be called a conscious process, but they do not know that they are perceiving. Their perception is a conscious process in the sense that it is a process by which they are aware of, and so come to know of, the things around them. If an infant does not even know that there is

something there—although he may not know what it is—I do not think he can be said to *perceive* that thing, at least not in any straightforward sense. Or if a creature such as a fly cannot be said to realize that there is something in front of him, then he cannot be said to perceive it. Its perception is not genuine perception, but at best something like subliminal perception. Nevertheless perception may be said to be a conscious process in so far as it gives us knowledge of things, knowledge of the things perceived, even if it is not a conscious process in the sense of one where the perceiver knows that he is perceiving.

We need to distinguish between a conscious process in the sense of one *of* which we are conscious, one such that if it occurs we know that it occurs, and a conscious process in the sense of one *by* which we are conscious of, and so know of, various things. And just as we can distinguish between these two senses in which a process might be conscious, so we can distinguish two senses in which a being might be said to be conscious. In the first sense a being is conscious if he possesses processes of which he is conscious; in this sense being conscious involves being self-conscious. In the second sense a being is conscious if he carries on, performs, processes *by* which he is conscious, even though he is not conscious of those processes; in this sense being conscious does not involve being self-conscious. We might draw a distinction between a *conscious being*, one who is conscious in the second sense, and a *being who possesses consciousness*, one who is conscious in the first sense.

Now all of this counts against my argument that perception is always and necessarily a conscious process and, as such, one that the perceiver necessarily knows of if it occurs.

For we can now see that although perception may always and necessarily be a conscious process in some sense, it is not always and necessarily a conscious process in the sense of one that the perceiver necessarily knows of if it occurs. This means that a conscious process is not necessarily something which is, qua conscious, known; its existence or occurrence does not have to be known before it can be said to exist or occur. It seems, then, that 'Because I am' cannot, after all, be a sufficient answer to the question 'How do I know that I am perceiving?' For the cat perceives without knowing that it does.

Perhaps the best way of coming at this is to ask: What is the difference between the cat and me such that I cannot perceive without knowing that I do, while the cat can? The answer is, I think, not that I possess some special way of knowing that the cat does not, but simply that I am more intelligent, that I am capable of reflecting on what I do in a way that the cat is not. For if the cat perceives, is conscious of, the mouse then he is in a position to know that he perceives it, every bit as much as I am in a position to know that I perceive it. If by knowledge we mean justified true belief then if the cat believed that he perceives the mouse his belief would be both true and justified, and hence would qualify as knowledge. The only trouble is that the cat doesn't believe it. Not that he believes it is false; he doesn't believe, or think, anything about it at all.

We might be tempted to put this by saying that seeing a mouse provides one with all the evidence necessary for inferring that one is perceiving, and that the difference between the cat and me is that I am capable of drawing this inference while the cat is not. But that would be misleading.

First, it is obvious that in fact I seldom if ever infer from seeing something that I see it. And second it is not clear that there is any inference to be drawn. What is this evidence that enables me to infer that I see a mouse? That a mouse is seen? But a mouse can be seen without its being true that *I* see a mouse. And it would be odd to suggest that I infer that I see a mouse from the fact that a mouse is seen by me. Rather, seeing a mouse entitles me to say that I see a mouse; there is nothing from which I infer, or need to infer, it.

However, the main point is that the special feature of conscious processes such as perception is not so much that if one perceives one must know that one does, but rather that if one perceives one must be in a position to know that one does. If I do not avail myself of this position that is, so to speak, my own fault, or at any rate the fault of my capacities and capabilities. Even so I am going to ignore this qualification, this fact that 'The conscious is, qua conscious, known' is not quite true as it stands. For the epistemological question 'How do I know?' is not the question of how or whether I happen to have learnt some fact, but rather the question of what sort of thing provides the justification that turns true believe into knowledge. And what justifies me in thinking that I perceive, and so provides me with knowledge that I do perceive, is the fact that I perceive. So, on a third look, 'Because I am' does turn out to be a sufficient answer to the epistemological question 'How do I know that I am perceiving?' But although the fact that I am perceiving explains *how* I know that I am, it does not mean *that* I do know it. Whether I know it, as I am in a position to, depends on empirical, not theoretical, considerations, in particular on my intelligence and ability to form beliefs about what I am doing.

3. I return to my original claim that the special feature of our knowledge of our conscious processes, and our special privilege in knowing these things, consists simply in the fact that for something to count as a conscious process in the first place its existence or occurrence must be known by the person whose consciousness it is. In the course of his attack on traditional doctrines of self-knowledge Ryle explicitly rejects the theory that the 'contents of consciousness' are, as he puts it, 'self-intimating', 'phosphorescent, like tropical sea-water, which makes itself visible by the light which it itself emits'.[1] This would seem to be the theory I am arguing for, although I do not claim that everything mental is 'self-luminous' since I do not claim that everything mental is a conscious state or process. Let us consider Ryle's objections.

His first point is that there are no mental happenings, no occurrences taking place in a second-status world, to be conscious or self-luminous. My answer is that, whether we should talk about a 'second-status' world or not, there are occurrences—such as perceiving and thinking—which are, in a definite sense, ghostly. I hope to have done something to explain what that sense is. Ryle's second, merely persuasive, point is that, in fact, no one ever appeals to consciousness as a way of knowing something; we say that we know something because we remember, see, or hear it, but we never say that we know something because we are conscious. Now the reason why no one answers a question like 'How do you know that you are perceiving?' with 'Because I am conscious' is partly that the question is rather too silly to ask in the first place, and partly because the more specific answer 'Because I am perceiving' is more to the point. The

[1] *Concept of Mind*, p. 159.

third argument is that it is an abuse of the word 'know' to talk about knowing claps of thunder, yellow surfaces, and the like. This involves the common error of confusing what is perceived with the perception of it; what is supposed to be 'phosphorescent', known qua conscious, is not what we perceive, the clap of thunder or the yellow surface, but our perception of it. Nevertheless, it might be said, it is still an abuse to speak of knowing perception. But who is speaking of it? When I say that perception is, qua conscious, known, what I mean is that whenever one perceives one knows, or more accurately is in a position to know, that one does, and that involves no misuse of the word 'know'.

Ryle's fourth argument is that there is no contradiction in asserting that someone might fail to recognize his frame of mind for what it is. This is certainly true. Freud has made us familiar, if we were not before, with the man who thinks he is rightly critical of another's unearned success when we know he is jealous. Yet I think this supports my case, so long as we remember that although the conscious is, qua conscious, known the mental is not, qua mental, conscious. For how do we describe this man's jealousy, if not as unconscious? His jealousy would be conscious only if he *knew* he was jealous. Finally Ryle brings forward his usual infinite regress argument, but here I am afraid I do not follow him. The whole point of the 'phosphorescent' theory, as Ryle admits, is that there is nothing apart from the conscious process itself, nothing separate, which acquaints us with or gives us knowledge of that process. So the regress, the question of whether I am spotting the fact that I am deducing, etc., does not arise. But, on the other hand, the question of whether one knows that deducing must, in so far as it is conscious, be known is a perfectly legitimate question. Ryle, for example, does not know it.

4. It used to be held as unquestionable that just as each of us has various external senses which acquaint us with what is going on in the 'external' world, the world around us, so each of us possesses a faculty of inner sense or introspection which acquaints us with what is going on inside our minds. But now that the theory has been questioned it seems equally obvious that there is no such faculty or sense. A little reflection is enough to show that I don't have to look within myself or examine myself internally to discover that I feel an itch, that I am thinking about jam tomorrow, that I believe in the actual infinite. This theory of an inner sense is a classic example of a conceptual point being misinterpreted as a psychological one. For, as I have argued, the point is not that we have some special way of knowing of the existence or occurrence of conscious states and processes, but rather that it is a necessary, analytic, truth that we know of the existence or occurrence of our conscious states and processes. But even though there is no need to postulate a process by which we are each acquainted with the contents of our own consciousnesses, I think we can give some sense to the notion of introspection, considered as a way of examining the contents of our minds.

A first definition of introspection might be: attending to what is private in the way that pains, thoughts, perception, etc., are. But this will not do, since, as we have seen, conscious processes are not private in the special sense (of mental privacy) that bodily sensations are, and although they are private in another sense (logical privacy) this is a feature they share with all processes. A better definition would be: attending to that which we have privileged access to.

Suppose I feel a pain. This is something to which I have privileged access, because unlike other people I do not have to find out that I feel the pain. A doctor or a psychologist or even myself might want to know more about the nature of my pain—how intense it is, whether it comes in waves, whether it seems to move, etc. To discover this I attend to what I feel. Here I am attending to something to which I have privileged access, and in doing this I am introspecting. The same applies when I am told to pay careful attention to my dreams, hallucinations, or after images.

It is less clear what I am to do if I am told to introspect my thinking. Presumably I must try to find out what precisely I do when I think, whether images are involved and in what ways, and so on. Once again I will be attending to what I have privileged access to. Similarly if I am told to introspect my perception this might be taken as an invitation to examine those private mental entities which, according to some theories, are all that we ever perceive. But even if these theories are discarded in favour of a common-sense Realism, according to which what we perceive are, usually, physical objects, physical sounds, physical smells, etc., we can still give a sense to introspecting what we perceive. This will be a matter of attending to how what we perceive looks to us, from our particular point of view, in our particular psychological and physiological state. This too is something to which we have privileged access. Not that it is impossible for the same things to look precisely the same to someone else. What I have privileged access to is not its having a certain appearance, but rather that this is how it looks, appears, *to me*. Others can tell how it looks to me by, for example, getting into the same position and checking that there are no physical or psychological differences between us. But I do not have to find out, in this or any other way, that this is how it looks to me. All I do is notice that this is how it looks.

Ryle has argued that introspection might best be replaced by the notion of retrospection, of looking back or remembering how it was as opposed to looking in and seeing how it is. I don't see that there is any need for this substitution with most of the cases I have mentioned, although there may be a case for it so far as introspecting one's thinking is concerned. For it would seem difficult both to think carefully about something and, at the same time, attend to that thinking. It does seem that we have to switch our attention from one to the other, from what we are thinking about to our thinking about it.

5. Ryle also remarks, 'Retrospection will carry some of the load of which introspection has been nominated for the porter. But it will not carry all of it, and in particular it will not carry many of the philosophically precious or fragile parcels' (*Concept of Mind*, p. 167). He is referring to the alleged infallibility and incorrigibility of introspection that has endeared it to so many who are in search of the absolutely certain. And perhaps it is worth pointing out that nothing I have said commits me to the view that 'introspection', or more generally our knowledge of our own minds, is infallible or incorrigible. To say that a person cannot think or perceive without knowing that he does is not to say that whenever he thinks he is thinking or perceiving it follows that he is thinking or perceiving. I have argued

elsewhere (*Perception and Our Knowledge of the External World*, Allen & Unwin) that a person can be mistaken about the nature of his bodily sensations, and about the nature of what he 'immediately' perceives, his sense data. Presumably he can also be mistaken about what goes on, what he is doing, when he is thinking. What is more debatable is whether he can be mistaken about the existence of his bodily sensations or sense data, and about whether he is perceiving—or thinking—at all.

The question is: can I think, believe, that I am thinking, perceiving, feeling a pain, when in fact I am not? It seems to me that so far as perception, including feeling bodily sensations, goes, I can be mistaken. A man suffering from attacks of blindness may, at a certain moment, not be sure whether he is perceiving or not; a lunatic may think he hears the voice of God when in fact he hears nothing, not even an hallucination, he just thinks he is hearing things; a man in great fear of torture may scream when he thinks the screws have been turned when as yet they haven't been (cf. 'For a moment I thought he had really hurt me'). Indeed it is worth asking what would have to be the case before it would be logically impossible to be mistaken over something. It seems that this could happen only where the truth of the thing in question is determined by what the person thinks it is. Obviously my thoughts are determined by what I think, so it follows that the one thing we cannot be mistaken about is what we are thinking. I may, to be sure, think that in thinking about the prediction of human actions from the courses of the stars I am thinking about astronomy, when in fact this is to think about astrology. But my mistake is to think that what I am thinking about *is called* 'astronomy'. I cannot be mistaken in thinking that I am thinking about a certain topic, which I mistakenly refer to as astronomy. Nor, for that matter, can I be mistaken in thinking that I think the topic is called astronomy. So, as Descartes discovered long ago, there seems to be only one thing that I cannot be mistaken about, viz. the fact that I am thinking. It is sometimes[1] suggested that the special feature of the Cartesian 'I think' is simply that this statement is self-guaranteeing, has to be true before it can be made, and that it is therefore no different from, say, 'I am using words' or 'I am here'. But although this may be fair comment on the conclusion 'I think' as Descartes reaches it, there is more to it than this. For not only must the statement be true if it is to be made, but also and more importantly whether it is made or not it cannot be true without our knowing that it is.

However, the fact that a man cannot be mistaken about what he is thinking does nothing to support the claim that introspection, at least in the sense explained, is infallible. For it is not by introspection, by examining myself or attending to anything, that I know what I am thinking. Where I may have to introspect, attend to what I am doing, is when I want to find out what happens when I think about some topic. And here my introspection may very well go wrong.

Finally, just as introspection is not infallible it is not incorrigible either. Just as it is possible for me to be mistaken about the nature of my pain, about how things look to me, about what happens when I think, so it is possible for others to correct me when I describe these things. Of course the fact that I have privileged access to them does mean that it is difficult, perhaps even presumptious, for you to contradict me. But it is possible.

[1] For example Ayer, *Problem of Knowledge* (Penguin), pp. 46 ff.

CHAPTER III

Our Knowledge of Other Minds

1. THE other minds problem can take many different forms: how do I know what you are perceiving, what you are thinking, that what you see looks like what I see, that you are thinking or perceiving at all, that you are conscious in the first place? It is worth remembering that as well as the philosophical problems there are also practical problems about our knowledge of other minds. Often we do not know what a person is thinking, or whether he did see what he claimed to see, and often we never find out. It would be a mistake to approach the philosophical problem in the hope that we might discover some way of answering these practical questions. The philosophical examination of our knowledge of other minds will never add to that knowledge. Nor, for that matter, will it subtract from it—although this is more likely to be disputed. The most that it will do, what it is supposed to do, is add to our understanding of the nature of that knowledge, explain what sort of knowledge it is, and how it differs from other knowledge.

It can be argued that we can never know what is going on 'in the mind' of another person, that there is no knowledge of other minds at all. Although I do not accept the argument, this is the point from which the philosophical discussion can best begin. For even if we insist, as I do, that we can and do know the minds of others, other minds scepticism may still have a point. When the sceptic claims that we cannot know his argument is, typically, not that what we claim to know is false, but that our knowledge of it is, in some way, inadequate. This inadequacy is measured and marked by contrasting our knowledge of other minds with other types of knowledge. So the sceptic can best be thought of as saying not what is false, that we cannot know the minds of others, but rather what may well be true, that our knowledge of other minds is, in some important respects, unlike, and the sceptic would say not as good as, our knowledge of certain other things. Thus other minds scepticism can be characterized as the lament that our knowledge of other minds is not as it could, and perhaps should, be.

For example, a typical sceptical lament is that a certain type of knowledge is not like our knowledge of mathematics, i.e. it is not absolutely certain in the sense that what is known must be true, cannot be false. The other minds lament could be that even if it is true that Jim sees the bull it might have been false, and so my knowledge that he sees it is not, in the required sense, absolutely certain. But, the reply is, this lament is pointless, in that knowledge of fact cannot be like knowledge of necessary truths; the facts might always be other than they are, so there is no point in lamenting that our knowledge of facts is not like our knowledge of necessary truths. Moreover, this sceptical lament has no special application to our knowledge of other minds; it does not serve to distinguish our knowledge of other minds from our knowledge of other matters of fact.

A more specifically other minds lament would be that we cannot know about other minds in the way that we know about the physical world. We know facts about physical objects, physical sounds, physical smells, etc., from what we perceive, but, the suggestion is, we can never perceive the minds, or what goes on in the minds, of others. One answer to this is to point out that not all our knowledge of physical things comes from perceiving the actual things in question. Most of my knowledge about physical things comes not from perceiving those things themselves, but from perceiving other things which inform me about them. So, in the same way, why should not my knowledge of the minds of others come from my perceiving other things, their words and actions for example, which inform me about what is going on in their minds? I know that Brutus killed Caesar not because I saw it happen, but because I saw it in a book. Similarly why should I not know that Fred is thinking about the Budget not because I see his thinking, but because he tells me he is thinking about it?

The sceptic's reply is that an item I perceive informs me, gives me knowledge about, some other thing which I do not perceive only in so far as it is possible to establish some sort of correlation between things of the first sort and things of the second sort. It is only in so far as the book is reliable that its saying that Brutus killed Caesar counts as giving me the knowledge that Brutus killed Caesar. And, says the sceptic, this is just what is not possible in the other minds case. If Fred's saying he is thinking about the Budget is to give me knowledge that he is, we have first to establish a correlation between his saying that he is thinking and the fact that he is, i.e. we must establish that his claims about what he is thinking are, usually or always, accurate. But this we cannot do, at least not by an appeal to what we perceive. So the fact that we cannot perceive the minds of others does make a difference to our knowledge of those minds. It means that our evidence-based beliefs about the minds of others cannot be checked by a direct appeal to those minds, as our evidence-based beliefs about objects we do not perceive can, at least in principle, be checked by a direct appeal to those objects.

We will have to come back to this, but the point for the moment is that our knowledge of other minds is different from our knowledge of the physical world, in that we cannot perceive the minds of others in the way that we can and do perceive the physical world. We can agree that it is from what we perceive that we acquire knowledge about other minds, that the answer to 'What provides us with knowledge about the minds of others?' is 'What we perceive', but the fact remains that our knowledge of other minds is not based on what we perceive in quite the way that our knowledge of the physical world is.

Is this difficulty, this impossibility of perceiving the minds of others, a factual or a logical difficulty? If it is only an empirical impossibility, if it is possible in principle but not in fact to perceive the minds of others, then the sceptical lament will have a definite force. The lament will be that we are not provided with a way of knowing the minds of others which we might have had. But if the impossibility is logical there will be no real point to the sceptic's lament. He will simply be regretting what he could not possibly have.

Now if by the 'contents of our minds' we do mean such things as perceiving and thinking then it is clear that the impossibility is logical. We cannot conceive what it would be like to perceive perceiving, or to perceive a thought. The idea that the minds of others might be perceptible, if only we had the equipment, is a result of the error of thinking that it is by some at least quasi-perceptual method that a person knows the contents of his own mind. Thus Wisdom (*Other Minds*, Blackwell, p. 226): 'The peculiarity of the soul is not that it is visible to none but that it is visible only to one.' If this were the case the other minds sceptic would have a good point. For in one case, our own, our knowledge of minds would be like our knowledge of the physical world. What a pity it isn't like that in all cases, for if it is like that in one case it must be possible for it to be like that in others. The sceptic would not be lamenting a logical impossibility, but merely the fact that we lack something we might have had, the ability to perceive the minds of others as we perceive our own minds, and as we perceive the physical world. But I would disagree with Wisdom: the peculiarity of the soul is not that it is visible only to one but that it is visible to none. I do not perceive, nor do I know what it would be like to perceive, my thoughts and my perception. I perceive what I perceive, naturally, but I do not and could not perceive my perception of it.

Where talk of 'perceptible only to one' does apply is in the case of bodily sensations, after-images, and hallucinations. Here the sceptic is lamenting a definite possibility which is not fulfilled, the possibility that our nervous systems might be such as to acquaint us with pains and itches in the bodies of others just as it acquaints us with pains and itches in our own bodies. I have argued that if our nervous systems were different, if we could connect our own nervous system with the nervous systems of other people, then it would be possible to feel the bodily sensations of other people, and to feel them in their bodies. Much the same holds for after-images and hallucinations, at least in so far as the perception of these things is due to the stimulation of what we might call the 'input end' of the nervous system and not to the stimulation of the 'receiving end' in the brain. That is, if my seeing an after-image is due to stimulation of the retina, resulting in a 'message' being sent along the optic nerve to the brain, it should be possible for someone else, given that he is able to 'plug into' my nervous system, to receive that very 'message' from my retina, and so see my after-image. But if my seeing such an image is due to a neurologist's probing the optic centres of my brain there will be no such 'message' to intercept and so, apparently, it would not be possible for another to see my image, even if he were able to 'plug into' my nervous system.

Thus the other minds problem about bodily sensations differs from the problems about conscious processes. The difficulty with conscious processes is that, even in our own case, we cannot know about them by perceiving them as we can know about physical objects by perceiving them. For conscious processes are not the sort of thing that can be perceived in the first place. But the difficulty with bodily sensations is that although they can be perceived, and in our own case we know about them because we perceive them, we cannot, as a matter of fact, perceive the bodily sensations of other people. This difference is often concealed by two errors. First the mistake of thinking that we know the contents of our consciousnesses in some at least quasi-perceptual way; and second the mistake of confusing l-privacy with m-privacy, which has led many to argue that it is a logical, and not just a contingent, fact that we cannot feel the pains of others. What is a necessary, logical, fact is that you cannot own my pains, for ownership of pains, like the ownership of voices but unlike the ownership of cars or houses, is not logically transferable. But what I have envisaged here is not that we might *own* the pains of others but that we might *feel* the pains of others, that we might feel the pains which belong to, are located in the bodies of, other people.

2. I now turn to another form of the other minds lament, this time the lament that we cannot know the minds of others in the way that we know our own minds. This lament is, as we have seen, often assimilated to the previous one, through the mistake of thinking that we know our own minds in the way we know physical objects, viz. by perceiving them. But the point is that I know that I am perceiving or thinking not because I perceive or observe myself perceiving or thinking but rather because this knowledge is simply a logical consequence of the fact that I am perceiving or thinking. This means that in order for another to know of my thinking or perceiving as I do it would be necessary for him to do my thinking or perceiving. And that, clearly, is logically impossible, because thinking and perceiving are, as processes, l-private. You cannot do my thinking or my perceiving because what makes it *this particular* occurrence of thinking or perceiving is the fact that *I* am doing it; if someone else were to be thinking or perceiving it would, *ipso facto*, be another, numerically distinct, occurrence of thought or perception. So in order for another to know that I am thinking or perceiving in the way that I know it, it is necessary for him to be me. In lamenting that we do not know of the conscious processes of others as we know of our own the sceptic is, once again, lamenting a logical impossibility.

However, it has been suggested that there is a way of knowing the minds of others as we know our own, which would mean, of course, that this is not a logical impossibility after all. The suggestion is that we might know the minds of others via some form of telepathy. In discussion this possibility is often linked with another, that we might manufacture some type of machine which when connected with the brain of another would show what was going on in that person's mind. However, these two suggestions are in fact quite different. They are assimilated only because telepathy is thought of as a means of perceiving the minds of others in just the way that introspection is thought of as a means of perceiving one's own mind. As Wisdom puts it (*Other Minds*, p. 101), 'What we have in mind is an extension of the introspective faculty.' But we have seen that we do not discover the contents of our own minds via any quasi-perceptual process of introspection, and similarly telepathy is not a way of discovering the contents of other minds via any quasi-perceptual process. Rather it would be a way of learning what is going on in the mind of another from various thoughts, images, etc., in one's own mind. The suggested mechanical device, on the other hand, would provide a way of knowing the mind of another from what I perceive.

Let us begin with the mechanical device: suppose I were able to discover what Fred is thinking or feeling by examining what is recorded on a television screen attached to his brain. What differences would this make to our knowledge of other minds? None at all, except as a check against deceit. For our knowledge of what a person is thinking or feeling would then be, as it is now, based on what we

perceive, although based on what we perceive on the television screen as well as on what we perceive of his behaviour.
The important difference between our knowledge of other
minds and our knowledge of the physical world would still
remain, in that although our knowledge of the former would
be based on perception we would still be unable to perceive
the phenomena which this knowledge is knowledge of.
Only the crudest picture of the mind would suggest that
when a person thinks 'Ain't life grand' a plaque inscribed
'Ain't life grand' is set up in his mind and then surveyed, a
plaque which we might survey too by means of the television screen. Similarly the television screen would not
provide us with a way of knowing the contents of another's
mind as he knows them, for he knows what he is thinking,
etc., because he thinks it, and not from any form of perception. Nor would the television screen make any difference
to our knowledge of another's bodily sensations, unless it
became a way of actually feeling the pains, etc., located
in another's body, i.e. became a way of 'plugging into'
another's nervous system.

Telepathy, on the other hand, would provide us with a
new way of knowing the minds of others, and would help
us in our practical problems about what goes on in other
minds. It would provide us with a way of knowing what
is going on in other minds from what is going on in our
own mind. We have seen that this would not be a way of
knowing other minds as we can know physical objects, viz.
by perceiving them. Indeed even if telepathy were a form
of perception it would still not be a way of perceiving the
minds of others. For what we would be aware of would not
be the contents of other people's minds but rather various

thoughts and ideas in our own minds which would inform us about what was going on in those other minds. For this reason telepathy would not even provide us with a way of knowing another's bodily sensations in the way he knows them; it would not be a way of feeling another's bodily sensations but rather a way of telling from one's own sensations, or perhaps thoughts or images of sensations, that another is feeling various sensations. For the same reason telepathy would not provide a way of knowing the minds of others as we know our own minds. It would provide us with knowledge of other minds only in so far as we regarded certain contents of our own minds as providing evidence for the existence of various contents in other minds. That is, we would be using what is going on in our own minds as evidence for what is going on in the minds of others. Yet, I do not use anything as evidence for what is going on in my own mind. Naturally I will learn of the telepathic thoughts and images in just the way that I learn of the other contents of my mind, i.e. my knowledge of their existence will be a logical consequence, because a necessary condition, of their existence. But the thoughts and images I learn of in this way are not the contents of the mind they inform me about, they are contents of my own mind.

3. To sum up: Our knowledge of other minds differs both from our knowledge of physical objects and from our knowledge of our own minds. Like our knowledge of physical objects our knowledge of other minds comes from what we perceive—it is because I perceive what I do that I know that you feel a pain, are thinking about the election, see an amber light, etc.—but unlike our knowledge of physical

objects our knowledge of other minds does not and cannot come from perceiving those things which it is knowledge of. It would, however, be pointless to be worried by this difference, because it is not even logically possible for us to perceive the minds of others, or the contents of those minds. Even so the sceptic's lament may still be said to have a point, although not as a lament, in so far as it points out, however indirectly, how our knowledge of conscious processes is, of necessity, different from our knowledge of physical objects, physical sounds, physical smells—and, for that matter, bodily sensations.

Again, our knowledge of other minds differs from our knowledge of our own mind in that the former is based on what we perceive while the latter is a logical consequence of the existence of our own minds. Or more accurately: our knowledge of our own conscious processes is a logical consequence of the existence of those processes. Once again it would be pointless to be worried by this difference, because it is not even logically possible that we should know the minds of others as we know our own minds. For to do that we should have to be those other people! The most the sceptic has done is show how our knowledge of other minds is, of necessity, different from our knowledge of our own minds.

Finally, our knowledge of the bodily sensations of others is like our knowledge of our own bodily sensations, and like our knowledge of physical objects, in that it comes from perception, from what we perceive, but it is also unlike it in that it cannot come from actually perceiving those things which the knowledge is knowledge of. But this time the impossibility is not a logical impossibility. In lamenting the fact that my knowledge of your pains is not like my knowledge of my pains, or my knowledge of your face, the sceptic is lamenting that we do not have a way of knowing the sensations of others that, had our nervous systems been different, could have had.[1]

[1] I hope it is obvious how much this chapter owes to Wisdom's *Other Minds*, including the paper 'The Concept of Mind'.

CHAPTER IV

The Other Minds Problem

1. So far so good. But this is not the end of the other minds problem, it is only the beginning. For the other minds sceptic wants to say not just that our knowledge of other minds is different from our knowledge of other facts, but that it is somehow inferior to other knowledge, so inferior as not to count as knowledge at all. This alleged inferiority may turn out to be a matter of logic, as it turns out to be a matter of logic that empirical knowledge is not certain in the special way that mathematical knowledge is, so we may well hesitate to regard this inferiority as excluding knowledge of other minds from the realm of knowledge altogether. But nevertheless we cannot claim to have got clear about the nature of our knowledge of other minds until we have examined the sceptic's reasons for denying that this knowledge is knowledge at all, until we have investigated his argument that knowledge of other minds is somehow deficient as knowledge.

We saw that I know that another person is thinking, perceiving, feeling a pain, etc., not by perceiving his thinking, perceiving, feeling a pain, but by perceiving what he says and does. What he says and does is my 'evidence' for the fact that he is thinking, perceiving, feeling a pain. By 'evidence' for some fact I mean whatever it is that tells us that it is so, whatever it is that provides us with knowledge of that fact. Thus what I see is my evidence for the fact that there is a

picture on the wall; I know that there is a picture on the
wall because I see it there. But on the other hand my seeing
it is not evidence for the fact that I am seeing, even though
it is because I see it that I know that I am seeing. For my
seeing does not tell me, provide me with the knowledge,
that I am seeing. I have no evidence, in this sense, for the
fact that I am seeing, and I do not need any.

Now in the other minds case evidence is always, perhaps
necessarily, about something quite different from what the
knowledge is knowledge of. My seeing that there is a picture on the wall is 'direct' evidence that there is a picture on
the wall, in that I actually perceive what is supposed to be
the case. Again my perceiving an egg break when dropped
is direct though not conclusive evidence that eggs break
when dropped, in that once again I actually perceive an
instance of what is held to be the case. But with other minds
my evidence for the fact that, for example, he is thinking,
about the Budget never includes, never refers to, his thought
or thinking itself. The evidence is always something else—
his actions, words, body, or brain. This is, of course, because
thinking, unlike pictures or eggs, cannot be perceived in
the first place, but that is not the point for the moment.
The point is that in producing evidence, in explaining how
I know, that he is thinking about the Budget, I never refer
to his thinking at all. I always refer to something else, whereas in producing evidence for my claim about the picture on
the wall or the state of eggs when dropped I do refer to the
picture or to eggs.

We can sum this up by saying that my evidence that Jones
feels a pain is 'indirect' evidence. Not that there is anything
wrong with indirect evidence as such. My knowledge that

there are tigers in India, or a war in Vietnam, is based on indirect evidence in precisely the same way. I know that there are tigers in India, a war in Vietnam, not because I have perceived these things for myself, but because I have perceived other things which give me this information. Nevertheless it seems that such indirect evidence is evidence only if we can establish some connexion or correlation between those things that constitute the evidence and those things that the evidence is evidence of. If I know that there is a war in Vietnam because I read about it in the papers, then my reading it in the papers is my evidence that there is such a war. But if there were no correlation between what the papers say and what actually happens then my 'evidence' would be no evidence at all; what the papers say would no more provide me with knowledge that there is a war in Vietnam than the fact that science fiction stories tell me that there is life on Mars provides me with knowledge that there is life on Mars. So in order to establish that I do know that there is a war in Vietnam it seems that we have to establish that my evidence is evidence, that there is a correlation between what the papers say and what actually happens. Similarly it seems that in order to establish that I do know that Jones feels a pain, we have to establish that my evidence is evidence, that there is a correlation between what Jones says and does and the fact that he feels a pain.

We can hardly deny that, in fact, we all believe that there is such a correlation, that we all believe that when people groan and writhe they are feeling pains. Indeed we can go further and say that we all *know* that a person who is writhing and groaning does feel a pain. But the fact remains that this knowledge, indeed all our knowledge of other minds and all our ascription of conscious states and processes to other people, depends on this belief, which we might call 'the belief in other minds' or 'the other minds belief'. That is, it is only because we all share this belief, because we all believe that there is a correlation between what other people say and do and their conscious states and processes, that we accept what they say and do as evidence, as providing us with knowledge, that they possess various conscious states and processes. This point is simple and indisputable; indeed it seems to me to be tautologous.

Nevertheless this is the point which opens the door to other minds scepticism. For, the sceptic will say, this belief is one which could be mistaken. It could be the case that when other people writhe and scream they are not feeling pains at all, even that although they speak and act as they do, they are none of them conscious at all. Of course it might be said that part of what is meant by calling them 'people' is that they are conscious, feel pains, etc., like us, but we can avoid this objection by using the more neutral term 'being'. Notice too that all the sceptic need say, and if he is wise all he will say, is that this belief in other minds *could be* mistaken. He need not say that it is mistaken (for how could he prove that it is?), much less that we don't have the belief. To say that we might be mistaken is not to say that we are mistaken, and the sceptic's point is only that the other minds belief does not embody a necessary truth. At first sight this seems plausible enough; we will come back for a second look in Section 4 below.

The sceptic's next move is to argue that this belief, which could be mistaken, is not one which we can prove to be correct, at least not without assuming the very point at issue. To establish that there is a correlation between pain-behaviour or other observable physical and physiological states on the one hand, and feeling a pain or other conscious states and processes on the other, we would have to establish that when people display pain-behaviour they are feeling pains. But the only way in which we can establish that they are feeling pains is by reference to their behaviour, and other similar things such as wounds, brain-states, and the like. Thus the only way in which we can establish that when people display pain-behaviour they are feeling pains is by accepting it as true that when they display pain-behaviour they are feeling pains. Which is, of course, to beg the question. So, the sceptic says, we cannot prove that there is a correlation, we cannot prove that our evidence is evidence, and from this it follows that our evidence is not evidence at all. The fact that Jones is bleeding and screaming does not tell me that he feels a pain, unless I can establish that when beings like him bleed and scream they are feeling pains. My position is precisely that of the man who does not know whether his newspaper is reliable; until it has been shown that it is he cannot know whether what it says is true.

This, then, is the sceptic's argument: Our knowledge about the minds, the conscious states and processes, of other people depends on our accepting what they say and do as evidence for the existence and nature of those conscious states and processes. But this evidence is indirect evidence, in the sense explained, and as such it should not be accepted as evidence at all until a connexion or correlation has been established between the evidence—what people say and do —and what it is evidence of—their conscious states and processes. Evidence is not evidence unless it can be proved to be evidence. But this connexion or correlation cannot be established, except by already assuming that there is such a connexion or correlation. Therefore our 'evidence' for facts about other minds is not evidence at all. Therefore our knowledge of other minds is knowledge without good grounds. Therefore it should not be accepted as knowledge at all.

It is worth repeating what the sceptic is not saying. He is not saying that we do not accept what other people say and do as evidence for 'what goes on in their minds'; he says rather that we should not accept it until we have proved that there is a connexion between the two. He is not saying that we are mistaken in thinking that there is this connexion between what people say and do and what goes on in their minds; he says rather that we cannot prove that we are not mistaken. He is not saying that other people do not think, perceive, feel pains; he says rather that inasmuch as we cannot show that our evidence that they do is evidence, we should not claim to know that they do. Notice finally that when the sceptic says that we cannot, in the last resort, prove the truth of our claims about other minds, he is not referring to the fact that our evidence that, for example, this man feels a pain does not entail that he does. If that were his argument then it would commit him to scepticism about much more than other minds and, consequently, would fail to bring out any special point about our knowledge of other minds. There are very few facts for which our evidence is, perhaps even can be, logically conclusive, and there seems no reason at all for insisting that evidence can be adequate only where it is logically conclusive.

2. As always the sceptic's conclusion—that we cannot have knowledge of other minds—is quite unacceptable. Whether or not someone is, in a certain situation, justified in the sense which is necessary for knowledge in regarding p as true depends on whether or not it is a situation of the sort ordinarily accepted as providing knowledge. So the fact that we would ordinarily say when we observe the man's behaviour that we know that he feels a pain shows that we are justified (in the sense which is necessary for knowledge) in believing that he does, whether it is possible to prove the point or not.[1] So something must be wrong with the sceptic's argument.

It might be said that the sceptic is simply wrong to describe the pain-behaviour as 'evidence' that he feels a pain. Certainly it can be argued—and we will discuss the argument in Chapter VI—that the pain-behaviour is more than evidence, but nevertheless it is evidence in the sense explained. It can scarcely be denied that it is his behaviour, including what he says, that tells us, that provides us with the knowledge, that he feels a pain. Again, it might be argued that we do not need to establish a correlation between this evidence and what it is evidence for, since we don't infer that the person feels a pain, we just see that he does.[2] Yet we can also see, in *The Times*, that income tax is going up again. For the argument to work what has to be shown is not that we can see that he feels a pain, nor that we see him when he feels a pain, but that we see his feeling the pain. And we can no more see his feeling the pain than we can see the income tax going

[1] For a more detailed discussion of this reply to the sceptic see my *Perception and Our Knowledge of the External World*, Chap. 10.

[2] On this argument see also Fodor and Chihara, 'Operationalism and Ordinary Language: A Critique of Wittgenstein', *American Philosophical Quarterly*, 1965, p. 282.

up again. The argument tends to trade on our not noticing a difference between feeling a pain and being in pain. Being in pain involves more than feeling a pain; it also involves visibly suffering from it. We can, therefore, see that a person is in pain in a way that we cannot see his feeling the pain. The question is whether seeing him suffer justifies our saying we see that he feels a pain, in the way that seeing it in *The Times* justifies our saying that we see that income tax is going up again. No doubt we are justified in both cases, but only because there is a correlation between what we see and what we say on the basis of what we see. The problem is whether we can prove that there is such a correlation.

The next move might be to try to prove that our other minds belief, our belief that there is this correlation between what people say and do and their having various conscious states and processes, is correct. But here it seems that the sceptic is right, that there is no proof. The only attempt that has had any currency at all is the traditional argument from analogy. This is the argument that we can establish that there is a correlation between observable behaviour and non-observable conscious states and processes by arguing, each of us, from our own case. I know that when I feel a pain I at least feel inclined to groan and wince, so I know that when Jones shows signs of groaning and wincing he too is feeling a pain. The objections are as well known as the argument. First, the argument proceeds from the smallest possible basis to the largest possible conclusion; it argues from one solitary instance to, perhaps, an infinity of cases. Secondly, as Wisdom puts it (*Other Minds*, p. 67), 'the analogy differs from other analogies in exactly the way which produces the original difficulty with regard to the knowing'.

That is, if, in an ordinary case, we are doubtful whether an analogy holds we can check up and see whether it does, but the whole point about other minds is that we can never test whether the analogy does hold.

I think most contemporary philosophers would agree that the sceptic is right about the impossibility of proving the correctness of our belief in other minds, or at any rate the impossibility of proving it in the way the sceptic demands. But they would tend to offer a different explanation of this fact: we cannot prove it not because it is an unjustifiable assumption, as the sceptic seems to suggest, but because it is not something that needs proof in the first place. There are two ways of arguing this. First, it can be said that the other minds belief is necessarily correct, in that what we believe is a necessary truth, and that therefore it does not require proof of the sort the sceptic has in mind. This is, in effect, to challenge the basic point from which the entire sceptical argument begins: the claim that the other minds belief could be mistaken. Or second, it can be said that the other minds belief is not one we could give up, not one we could doubt or deny, and therefore does not stand in need of proof. I will begin with the second of these suggestions.

3. The argument is that there is no need to prove what no one can doubt. As Wittgenstein puts it, considering the suggestion that our ascription of conscious states to others involves a 'presupposition': 'Doesn't a presupposition imply a doubt? And doubt may be entirely lacking. Doubting has an end' (*Philosophical Investigations*, Blackwell, p. 180). It may be possible, in principle if not in practice, to deny that the screaming man feels a pain, but that doesn't mean that

we have to prove that he does feel a pain. There is no need to prove it unless we can doubt it. We just cannot believe that the suggestion that he does not feel a pain is true. ' "But, if you are *certain*, isn't it that you are shutting your eyes in face of doubt?"—They are shut' (*Philosophical Investigations*, p. 224).

How far does this count against the sceptic? Let us take another example. We can, if we are sufficiently pedantic, say to ourselves as we sit in a room, 'Perhaps I am not really sitting here, perhaps I am in bed dreaming', but, unless there is something very odd about what we perceive, we cannot believe that this statement is true. One thing that this shows is that philosophical doubts are, in an obvious sense, idle. They make no difference to what we do, nor to what we believe is the case. Or if they do it is time we turned to some other subject. But apart from such side issues as Descartes's wish that we should proceed methodically in all our reasonings, philosophical doubts were never intended to make us act differently, to worry us about the existence of external objects or other minds. They were intended to reveal some fact or other about our knowledge, some feature of the status or nature of our knowledge of such things as external objects or other minds. Whether he realized it or not Descartes established once and for all that our knowledge of matters of empirical fact cannot be like our knowledge of, say, mathematics, because mathematics is certain in a way that matters of fact cannot be. The Cartesian doubt may have been idle in that it made no difference to how we act or think, but it did have a point, and a good one.

It has become fashionable to characterize philosophical doubt as absurd, usually for no other reason than that it is philosophical. This view rests on a misunderstanding. It would be true to say that philosophical doubt is not genuine doubt. Ordinarily to doubt p is to wonder seriously, to be uncertain, whether p is true, but when Descartes 'doubted' whether his body existed he did not, and could not, seriously wonder whether it did. There are limits to genuine doubt, and these limits are psychological not logical—one can, for example, genuinely wonder whether 255 divided by 17 is exactly 15. But philosophical doubt does not consist in seriously wondering whether some statement is true; it consists in 'questioning' the statement, considering whether it is true. The limits to this questioning, if it is to have a point, are logical, not psychological. In a sense one can question anything, even mathematics, but this questioning has a point only where the statement in question could be false. It might be said that it is misleading to refer, as Descartes did, to this questioning as doubt. But it matters little what we call it; the point is that it can be done.

Now if someone feels forced to *deny* that the things he perceives exist, then this is absurd, at least in that his denial has no rational justification. The fact that we could be mistaken doesn't mean that we are. It may well be absurd in an even stronger sense, i.e. incoherent, to hold that nothing we ever perceive exists, and in that case even the philosophical doubt would be absurd. But I am thinking of the more moderate claim that the things I perceive on a particular occasion, for example now, might not exist, that I might at this particular moment be dreaming. I am sure that I am not dreaming, and I find it impossible to take seriously the suggestion that I am, but for all that it could be so.

Again, if someone doubts in the ordinary sense, i.e.

genuinely wonders, whether the things he perceives exist
then this too is absurd, or at any rate abnormal and insane.
Clearly there is something seriously wrong with anyone who
genuinely believes that the things he perceives might not
really be there. But if someone doubts in the philosophical
sense, i.e. questions whether the things he perceives exist,
then this is not absurd. In so far as it is possible that the things
we perceive might not exist, so far it is possible to question
whether they do. Those who think that this questioning is
absurd, and that the philosopher is in need of a cure, have
confused him with one of three other people: the man who
genuinely thinks that they don't exist; the man who doesn't
know what to think; or the man who thinks he is doubting
in the first sense when in fact he is doubting in the second,
i.e. the man who questions the existence of what he perceives and thinks he is seriously wondering whether it does
exist. This last is the most interesting case. Perhaps Descartes
was in this position; certainly most of us get into it at one
time or another. What we need then is a good dose of
common sense which will bring home the absurdity—the
impossibility and the insanity—of doubting the existence of
what we see. But, and this is the main point, the perplexity
of which we are thus cured is not the philosophical perplexity. The fact that no man in full possession of his senses
can seriously wonder whether what he perceives exists is
no more philosophically relevant than the fact that it is possible for a poor mathematician like myself to wonder, quite
genuinely, whether 17 goes 15 times into 255. In fact those
who seek to cure the philosopher of his absurd perplexities
are making precisely the same mistake as those 'sceptics' who
think they can seriously wonder whether what they perceive

does exist. They make the mistake of confusing questioning, which is possible, with genuine doubt, which for most of us is not. The attempt to question our belief in the existence of what we perceive is not absurd, or even misguided: it is of immense importance to the theory of knowledge, and it was Descartes's great achievement to show that it can be done.

To return to feeling pains. Someone who genuinely wonders whether the screaming man feels a pain, someone who seriously believes (as opposed to merely contemplating the possibility) that he might not be, stands in need of a cure, though it should come from a psychotherapist rather than from a philosopher. Although not incoherent his belief is absurd to the point of insanity. Again a philosopher who claims that he seriously wonders whether the screaming man feels a pain is also in need of a cure, though presumably a philosophical cure. For he fails to see the difference between genuinely wondering whether something might be so, and merely contemplating the possibility. To question a fact is not really to doubt it; it was Descartes's mistake to think that if some thing could be false it must therefore be doubtfully true. So to think that what can be questioned is therefore subject to genuine doubt is absurd, unreasonable, and anyone who thinks this needs to be cured from his philosophical perplexity. But what is not absurd is to realize that the belief, the fact if you prefer, that these other beings are conscious as I am can be questioned, is capable of being false, even given that these beings act as I do.[1] Those who insist on this are not in need of any cure, and those who think that they

---

[1] In all of this I assume, with the sceptic, that the connexion between pain-behaviour and feeling a pain is a contingent one. Whether or not this is so is to be discussed in the next section.

are have made the same mistake as the man who thinks that the argument about other minds can make us genuinely unsure about the screaming man. They have confused philosophical doubt, questioning, with genuine doubt, seriously wondering whether some proposition is or is not true.

But even if the philosophical doubt is not absurd the original point, that there is no need to prove what cannot be doubted, may still hold good. If we cannot bring ourselves to take seriously the suggestion that the screaming man does not feel a pain then, the argument is, there is no need to prove that he does feel a pain. No doubt it is possible to question whether he does, in so far as it is logically or even empirically possible that he does not, but the fact that a statement could be false does not mean that we have to prove it true. It is enough that we are convinced that it is true: there is no need for proof until we have some reason for thinking it false.

Now if the sceptic were saying that the other minds belief is a belief that we cannot be sure about, and that since we are uncertain we should not claim to know what is going on in other minds—and perhaps some have wanted to say this —then the present point would show that he was wrong. But the scepticism I am discussing maintains only that we cannot prove that the belief is correct, except by assuming at some point in the argument the very point at issue. To say that in an actual case we cannot doubt for a moment, and that therefore there is no need of proof, may remove the complaint from the sceptic's tone of voice, but it does not show that he is mistaken. In fact the sensible sceptic will insist on this point himself. It is not difficult to imagine a Hume saying 'Thus the sceptic still continues to reason and believe about other minds even though he asserts that he cannot defend his reason by reason; and by the same rule he must assent to the principle concerning other minds, though he cannot pretend, by any arguments of philosophy, to maintain its veracity. Nature has not left this to choice, and has doubtless esteemed it an affair of too great importance to be trusted to our uncertain reasonings and speculations. We may well ask, What causes induce us to believe in the existence of other minds? but it is in vain to ask, Whether there be other minds or not? This is a point which we must take for granted in all our reasonings.'

All that has been said so far is that the sceptic is asking for the unnecessary, not that he is asking for the impossible. But it might be said that the sceptic is asking for the impossible. Then, surely, his scepticism will be absurd, and there will be no need to answer it? Personally I am not sure whether the sceptic is asking for the logically impossible. He is asking for a non-circular proof that these other beings around us are conscious as he is, and prima facie at any rate this demand is not incoherent in the way that the demand for a round square is. Certainly we are entitled to ask what sort of thing would satisfy the sceptic, what type of information he would accept as proving that these beings are conscious, but it is not clear whether the onus is on the sceptic to show that there could be such information, or whether it is on the anti-sceptic to show that there could not. If the sceptic complains that we lack the information then I suppose the onus is on him to explain what is lacking, but when the anti-sceptic maintains that the scepticism is absurd, then I think the onus is on him, the anti-sceptic, to show that it is absurd, that it does involve asking for the impossible.

So far as a person's thoughts are concerned there seem to be two ways in which I can know that a person is thinking. I can, where I am the person who is thinking, know it because I am doing the thinking, thinking being a conscious process. Or, if someone else is thinking, I can know this from his behaviour, what he says and does. So if there is no other way of knowing that another is thinking it is clear that the request for a proof, other than by reference to his behaviour, is a request for the impossible. What is not clear is whether it is a logical impossibility. The point seems only to be that we cannot think of an alternative, not that any alternative is logically impossible. The same applies if we are concerned to prove that other people feel pains. I have argued that it could be possible to feel pains in other people's bodies, but even if this did happen it would still be evidence only that there are pains in other people's bodies, and not evidence that those people themselves feel those pains.

But let us agree, for the sake of argument, that it is logically impossible to meet the demand for a non-circular proof that other beings think or feel pains. This would count against the argument that unless we can prove that other beings think, feel pains, etc., we should not claim to have knowledge of other minds. There is also the extra objection that the fact that we cannot prove that what we claim to know is true does not show that we do not know it; what is necessary is that what we claim to know is true, not that we can prove that it is true. But it would not count against the sceptical argument I am discussing. The argument sketched in Section 1 rested on the claim that we cannot prove the correctness of the other minds belief. To say that such a proof would be logically impossible is precisely to concede the sceptic's claim.

So far, then, the sceptic seems to have a point: although our belief in other minds is something we are absolutely convinced about, it is also something which we cannot prove to be correct, and this has important consequences for the nature of our knowledge of other minds. Just as showing that we cannot, logically cannot, know the minds of others as we know our own minds brings out a (necessary) difference between our knowledge of our own minds and our knowledge of other minds, so showing that we cannot, logically cannot, prove the correctness of the belief on which our ascription of conscious states to others is based brings out a (necessary) difference between our knowledge of other minds and our knowledge of other facts.

But all of this is so only given the original claim that the connexion between observable phenomena, like pain-behaviour, and non-observable conscious states and processes, like feeling a pain, is a contingent connexion, the claim that the fact that these two are connected is a fact that can be questioned. We have now to consider whether or not this is so.

4. We now return to the first of the two suggestions in Section 2 above, the suggestion that the other minds belief is not one that needs to be proved correct because, despite what the sceptic says, it is not one that could be mistaken. This suggestion is widely accepted. Sidney Shoemaker, for example, explicitly accepts the sceptic's argument, but stands it on its head and so rejects the basic premiss: 'Unless some relationships between physical and psychological states are

not contingent, and can be known prior to the discovery of empirical correlations, we cannot have even indirect inductive evidence for the truth of psychological statements about other persons, and cannot know such statements to be true or even probably true.'[1]

This is a revealing quotation. We do not want to accept the sceptical conclusion that we have no knowledge of other minds. We all know that the only way of avoiding the conclusion of a valid argument is by rejecting one or more of its premisses. So, if the cost of avoiding scepticism is allowing that the connexion between, for example, pain-behaviour and feeling a pain is a necessary one, then this is a price we will be willing to pay. But, as I shall argue in the next section, we do not need to pay this price; there is another, more acceptable, way out of the sceptic's argument. The point I want to make here is that the claim that the connexion is a necessary, conceptual, one is not, in itself, particularly plausible. At any rate the connexion is clearly not an analytic one. 'This being exhibits all the marks of feeling a pain, but does not actually feel one' is not self-contradictory, so if it is incoherent—if 'Those who exhibit pain-behaviour are feeling pains' is some form of conceptual truth—then it must be in some other, more subtle, way. There are, I know, powerful arguments for the view that the connexion is a necessary one, and I will be considering three of these in the next three chapters. My point here is that powerful arguments are needed; prima facie, at any rate, the connexion is a contingent, empirical, one.

---

[1] *Self-Knowledge and Self-Identity* (Cornell), pp. 167–8. This argument is not, of course, directed against the sceptic; it would be question-begging if it were.

The main reason for insisting that the connexion is a contingent one is obvious enough. Screaming, groaning, writhing, etc., are one thing, we want to say, and feeling a pain is another. No doubt the two are connected—presumably one is the cause of the other—but they are different and distinguishable. If there is a difference between feeling a pain and screaming, groaning, writhing, etc.—and surely there is—then it must be possible, at least in logic, to have the one without the other.

All the same screaming, groaning, writhing, etc., are referred to as 'pain-behaviour', and it might seem that there must be some conceptual link between pain and pain-behaviour. But this particular link holds only between the names, the labels, that we give the phenomena. There is a similar link between 'coffee' and 'the smell of coffee', but these two are still separable—we can have the smell of coffee produced by something else, and we can have coffee without the smell. The point is only that, because of certain contingent facts, the smell is known as the smell of coffee, although it might also be argued that the smell has to be identified in this way, that it is a necessary fact that we identify the smell by reference to the sort of thing that has that smell. Similarly it seems that pain and pain-behaviour are logically—even empirically—separable, that we can have pains without the behaviour, and vice versa. The point is only that, because of certain contingent facts, the behaviour is known as pain-behaviour, although it might also be argued that pains have to be identified via such behaviour, that it is a necessary fact that we identify the sensations by reference to the behaviour that goes with them.

So I do not think we have much difficulty in allowing that

a man might feel a pain without displaying any pain-behaviour, or that a man might display pain-behaviour without feeling a pain. In fact it is easy to think of cases where just this happens. But it might be said that this is to take far too restricted a view of the 'observable phenomena' which constitute our evidence, provide us with the knowledge, that another feels a pain. It is also relevant to consider whether he has been wounded, whether he is an actor on a stage, whether he looks as though he is holding something back, fighting a temptation to groan or wince, and so on. And, of course, we should also consider what he says. What tells us whether another feels a pain is not just what he does, but also what he says, and the whole context of his words and deeds. So we have to show not just that it is logically possible for a man to feel a pain without showing pain-behaviour, and vice versa, but that it is logically possible for a man to show all the characteristic marks of feeling a pain and yet not be feeling one. This seems more difficult. The question at issue is: could a person be, in all possible observable respects, precisely like someone who was feeling a pain, and yet not be feeling a pain?

Although the sceptic's position now seems less plausible than if we talk merely about the connexion between, say, groaning and feeling a pain, I still think the sceptic is right. In an actual case the fact that a man shows all the characteristic marks of feeling a pain does establish that he feels a pain, but this is only because we have the other minds belief in the first place, because we all believe that when people groan, etc., and there is nothing to suggest that they are not feeling a pain, then they are in fact feeling pains. But suppose it is suggested that a being that we think of as another person is really nothing but a humanoid robot, equipped with the 'correct' responses to wounds and stabs, right down to a language in which to report and describe the pains it claims to feel. The suggestion is completely unverifiable, and there is no reason whatsoever for regarding it as correct, but unless we are tempted—as we often are in these matters—to a verification theory of meaning, this does not make the suggestion senseless or incoherent. In so far as the suggestion makes sense, in so far as it is logically possible for the suggestion to be correct, so far it is possible for other beings to display all the marks of feeling pains that they do display, and yet not be feeling pains. Personally I think there is good reason for regarding the suggestion as false; we can regard it as false until we have an explanation of how these beings come to report and describe pains as they do. A possible explanation—that this might be a skilful piece of computer programming—is not itself an explanation. But even if the suggestion is false, as I am sure that it is, it makes sense, it could be true, and that is all the sceptic needs. A different, but related, argument—that we cannot rule out all the possibilities in advance—leads Malcolm to a similar conclusion: 'The criteria for the use of third-person psychological statements are not related to the latter by an entailment-relation.'[1]

This far-fetched, but apparently coherent, suggestion that another might display all the usual marks of feeling a pain and yet not be feeling one has to be distinguished from another suggestion which is incoherent: that another might display all the usual marks of feeling a pain without what he feels being a pain. It is sometimes suggested that even if

[1] *Knowledge and Certainty* (Prentice-Hall), p. 115. I discuss this argument on p. 120 below.

the Martians, for example, reacted to wounds and stabs precisely as we do, this would not show that they felt *pains*. Despite their pain-behaviour they might be feeling not pains but (what we would call) heat sensations, or perhaps something totally unlike what we feel. This suggestion *is* incoherent; we will see in Chapter V that what makes a sensation a pain sensation is that it is produced by wounds and stabs, is accompanied by groans and winces, and so on. So it is a self-contradiction to suggest that what a man feels when he is wounded and reacts in the characteristic way might not be a pain. However, the sceptic can admit that what the wounded, groaning man feels, if he feels anything, must be a pain; what he questions is not what the sensation felt will be, but whether a sensation is felt in the first place.

There is a further suggestion that might be made: that the pains I feel may be totally unlike the pains some other being feels. The fact that the sensation is caused in a certain way and that I react to it as I do establishes, as a matter of definition, that it is a pain. But the fact that our sensations are caused in the same way, and that we both react to them in the same way, does not establish, at any rate not as a matter of definition, that what we feel is alike in any other respects. This third suggestion is unverifiable and consequently idle, but not prima facie incoherent—although there is the argument that, contrary to appearances, it is unstatable.

Notice too that allowing that there might be cases where though a being displayed all the usual marks of feeling a pain he did not actually feel one, does not conflict with the fact that in any particular case we would find it impossible to believe that he was not feeling a pain. I might find it impossible to believe of any individual student that he had been cheating, and yet be absolutely convinced that one of them has been. This amounts only to allowing that there is one case where, despite my convictions, I am mistaken. Similarly there is no difficulty in allowing that there might be cases where, despite our convictions, we are mistaken in thinking that a certain being feels a pain.

I have been arguing that the sceptic's claim, that the connexion between observable phenomena such as pain-behaviour and conscious states and processes such as feeling a pain is a contingent one, is prima facie quite plausible. If it is not a contingent connexion then it has to be shown that it is not, and in the chapters that follow we will look at the three main arguments for holding that it is not. Nevertheless there is a tendency to take it for granted that the connexion is not contingent, that the sceptic's claim is absurd. Perhaps my best argument for showing that it is not obviously absurd is that, until quite recently, philosophers have always thought of the connexion as contingent. But there are, I think, three reasons why some philosophers find this as obviously absurd as I find it plausible. First, there is a failure to separate the psychological fact that we cannot in a particular case bring ourselves to doubt that the being feels a pain from the logical fact that it is still possible that the man does not. The very word 'absurd' conceals this distinction. Normally 'absurd' means not so much incoherent, as unbelievable: 'That's absurd' often amounts to 'You don't expect me to believe that?' But the fact that a statement is absurd in this sense does not mean that it is self-contradictory or incoherent. The claim that the world is flat—that it only seems round because of the influence of para-gravitational forces, the effect of atmospheric conditions on photographs taken from rockets, and so on—is absurd in the sense of unbelievable, but 'The world is flat' contains no conceptual absurdities.

Second, there is the fear that once we accept the sceptic's point we will be forced to the sceptic's conclusion that we cannot have knowledge of other minds. Since this conclusion is felt to involve some form of conceptual absurdity, in particular a misuse of the word 'know', it is felt that the claim that a man might display all the usual marks of feeling a pain and yet not feel one must also involve a conceptual absurdity. There are two things to be said about this. First, as we shall see, it allows too much force to the sceptic's argument, as if the conclusion follows the moment the premiss is conceded. Secondly, even though the conclusion is false it does not involve a conceptual absurdity. 'We do not know **that** other people feel pains' is false, but it is not incoherent. It could be true, e.g. in a world in which there were no pains at all, cf. 'We do not know that other people execute volitions (for the simple reason that other people do not execute volitions).' What is wrong with the claim that we do not know that other people feel pains is the suggestion that something which ordinarily qualifies as knowledge is not knowledge after all. This is to say that an ordinarily accepted use of 'know' is a misuse, when a misuse is precisely one which conflicts with the ordinarily accepted use. The conceptual absurdity lies not in 'We do not know that other people feel pains', but in the claim that what we all allow as knowledge is not knowledge, even if the truth of what we claim to know were granted.

Third, we feel inclined to say that if, for example, lying groaning in a pool of one's own blood does not count as being in pain then it is difficult to see what does. To some extent this point depends on talking about 'being in pain' rather than about 'feeling a pain', because, as we have seen (p. 49 above), being in pain seems necessarily to involve pain-behaviour in a way that feeling a pain does not. But even if we replace 'being in pain' by 'feeling a pain' there is still something to the point. Wittgenstein, in particular, has insisted that it is only in so far as a thing can speak, act, etc. as we do that we can think of it as being conscious, feeling pains, and so on. We can, of course, *say* that a pot or a stone feels a pain, but this form of words remains quite empty until we can think of the pot or stone as acting and speaking (*Philosophical Investigations*, §§ 281–4). But to insist that we cannot sensibly say, that we cannot really understand what is meant by saying, that a thing feels a pain unless that thing is at least capable of displaying the characteristic marks of feeling a pain, is not to say that to display these marks is to feel a pain. It is only when a thing displays pain-behaviour that we can think of it as feeling a pain, but this does not mean that its feeling a pain follows from the fact that it displays this pain-behaviour.

So far, then, we can agree with the sceptic that the connexion between pain-behaviour and the like and actually feeling a pain is not a necessary, or at any rate not an analytic, one. Indeed the sceptic's point seems even more obvious if we consider conscious states or processes other than our awareness of pains. Those who argue that there is a necessary conceptual link between observable phenomena and conscious states and processes make their task seem easier than it is by concentrating on a case where there is a specially distinctive type of behaviour almost universally associated with the particular conscious state. But if I suspect someone of thinking about how best to murder his wife there is no way in which I can establish that that is what he is doing, certainly no way which establishes it as a matter of logic. It might be said that this is not a genuine objection, since it is a straightforward matter of fact that I just do not know whether he is thinking about how best to murder his wife. There may be a practical problem here, but it is not a philosophical one. The philosophical problem is raised by the sceptic's claim that we do not know what we all ordinarily claim to know, and in this case we do not claim to know —or if we did it would only be because we have observed some behaviour which is linked with thinking about that in just the way that pain-behaviour is linked with feeling a pain.

This may be an adequate reply for the moment, but if it is possible for a person to think about how best to murder his wife without displaying anything which can be linked conceptually with thinking about it, then it follows that there must be something wrong with any argument which maintains that we cannot ascribe conscious states to others except on the basis of observable behaviour which is conceptually linked with those conscious states. Perhaps it can be shown that we cannot know that another possesses a certain conscious state, except by reference to that person's observable behaviour, but it cannot be shown that we cannot *say* it except by reference to the behaviour. This seems to me to confirm the sceptic's claim that the link between behaviour and conscious state is an evidential, not a conceptual, one.

5. Suppose we do accept the sceptic's claim that the connexion between, for example, feeling a pain and pain-
behaviour is a contingent one. What then of the sceptic's
argument, sketched on pp. 46–47 above? It seems to me that
the correct point at which to challenge this argument is at the
claim that evidence is not evidence unless it can be proved
to be evidence. That is, we might argue that for something
to count as evidence, to provide us with knowledge, about
something else, what is necessary is only that there be some
correlation between the two, and not that we be able to
demonstrate that there is a correlation. The sceptic does not
deny that there is a correlation between observable phenomena and conscious states; he says only that we cannot prove
that there is. But so long as there is a correlation, is this not
enough for the observable phenomena to count as evidence
to provide us with knowledge? What is necessary is not that
we prove that there is a correlation, but that we all agree
that there is one. We all do agree that a person's behaviour
constitutes evidence, provides us with knowledge, that he
possesses various conscious states and processes, so we all
agree that we do have knowledge of other minds.

This may seem to concede too much to the sceptic. If we
concede that we cannot prove the correctness of this other
minds belief on which our ascription of conscious states and
processes to others is based, we seem to concede that our
knowledge of other minds is, in a definite sense, deficient.
We may still want to call it knowledge, but if it is, as the
sceptic argues, based on evidence which we cannot prove
to be evidence, this does mean that our knowledge of other
minds does not 'measure up to' various other types of knowledge. This, of course, is the basic point—I would say the

basic truth—that underlies the sceptic's argument. We can think of the sceptic as presenting us with a challenge, as asking us to justify our calling knowledge of other minds knowledge at all, when it differs in this important respect from other knowledge. No doubt we will continue to call it knowledge no matter what the sceptic says, but his argument may lead us to wonder how far we are justified in speaking like this.

The fundamental point is that our knowledge of other minds is and must be different, in certain important respects, from other types of knowledge. Indeed this should have been obvious from the beginning. It seems perfectly clear that our knowledge of other minds, and the certainty which goes with it, is different, logically not psychologically, from our knowledge of other types of fact. Wittgenstein saw this, in a way that some of his followers do not, when he said (*Philosophical Investigations*, p. 224), 'I can be as *certain* of someone else's sensations as of any fact. But this does not make the propositions "He is much depressed", "$25 \times 25 = 625$" and "I am sixty years old" into similar instruments. The explanation suggests itself that the certainty is of a different *kind*.—This seems to point to a psychological difference. But the difference is logical.'

What is more disputable is whether the sceptic's point does pose a problem for us. Do we have to explain why we accept, as we obviously do, observable phenomena such as other people's words and behaviour as evidence, as providing us with knowledge, about other minds? Notice that the problem is not supposed to be that of explaining why we all accept the other minds belief, of explaining how we come to have that belief in the first place. These are, presumably, psychological questions. The philosophical question is why we should accept knowledge of other minds as knowledge when it differs in this important respect from other knowledge.

It seems that Wittgenstein would not accept this as a genuine problem, even though he accepts the sceptic's point on which it is based. For, Wittgenstein would say, the fact that we accept knowledge of other minds as knowledge is not something that can be or needs to be justified. We can justify some of the things we say by reference to linguistic procedures, but we cannot justify the linguistic procedures themselves; all we can say is, 'The language-game is played'. 'The chain of reasons has an end', 'What people accept as a justification—is shown by how they think and live' (*Philosophical Investigations*, §§ 326, 325). This rejection of the problem raises issues too broad for us to go into here. I will say merely that it seems to me a counsel of despair. I believe it should be possible to explain why we say what we do, and in particular I think we can provide a justification for our claim to have knowledge of other minds. Indeed I think the justification emerges from Wittgenstein's own teachings.

From any practical point of view we are, of course, fully justified in accepting what other people say and do as evidence for what goes on in their minds. If people in general did not allow that other beings were conscious in the way that they themselves are, life would be solitary, poor, nasty, brutish, and above all short. If I personally were not prepared to allow that other people are conscious like me, I would, no doubt, live out my days in one kind of an institution or another. Most important of all is the point that, whatever the philosophers say, I cannot possibly bring myself to take seriously the suggestion that what others say and do is not evidence for what goes on in their minds. The question is whether our accepting this as evidence admits of a *theoretical* justification.

This is *the* other minds problem. It has a solution, and in fact its solution provides the basis for those arguments which attempt to undercut this entire discussion, those arguments which seek to establish that the connexion between observable phenomena and conscious states is not a contingent one, that when the sceptic suggests that there might be all the usual marks of feeling a pain without a pain being felt, what he says is, if not self-contradictory, incoherent in some other way. The correct answer to the other minds problem will best emerge by a criticism of these mistaken attempts at solving, or dissolving, the problem. Each of these arguments—the private language argument, the argument from criteria, and the argument from persons—is based on an important insight into the other minds problem, but I will argue that they all go too far, that they all try to establish more than can be established. My discussion in the next three chapters will be mainly negative, but I trust that the positive point will emerge.

CHAPTER V

The Private Language Argument

1. THE sceptic tries to drive a wedge between pain-behaviour and feeling a pain, claiming that it is always possible to have the one without the other. The private language argument hopes to show that this wedge cannot be driven, that we cannot even speak about feeling a pain except by reference to pain-behaviour, and that therefore what the sceptic tries to say cannot be said. The private language argument hopes to show this by showing that a private language is impossible, but unfortunately it is never made clear what precisely a 'private language' is supposed to be. We can distinguish at least four things:

(1) A language which, as it happens, only one person does use and understand. ✗ *see* 243 P I.

(2) A language which, as it happens, only one person can use and understand.

(3) A language which, as a matter of logic, only one person can use and understand.

(4) A language in which terms refer to 'private objects', items of which only one person is and can be aware, e.g. bodily sensations.

Private languages of the first type, what we might call 'accidentally private' languages, are of little concern to us, and it is perfectly obvious that there can be such languages, for example, the private code in which a person keeps his diary. Discussions of the possibility of a private language often take the form of asking whether a language-less Robinson Crusoe could or could not develop a language for himself. This seems both irrelevant and easy to answer. For so long as it is allowed, as it usually is, that the language could be learnt by others then it would be merely an accidentally private language, and it seems clear that such languages are possible. Wittgenstein, for one, allowed their possibility (*Philosophical Investigations*, § 243). Nevertheless the possibility of Crusoe's inventing a language for himself is very different from the possibility of my inventing a private code. One way of arguing that there cannot be a necessarily private language would be to argue that any accidentally private language must be parasitic on some previously understood public language, as my code is parasitic on English. For if you cannot develop a private language except by reference to a public language, there cannot be a necessarily private language. Any private language could be learnt by translating it back into the public language by reference to which it had been developed. But on the other hand, to argue that Crusoe could develop a language all by himself is not to show that there can be a necessarily private language. It is only to destroy one line of argument aimed at showing that there cannot be.

Next, the distinction between private languages of the second and third types does not matter for our purposes, so I will refer to them both as 'necessarily private' languages. What is important is the distinction between such necessarily private languages, and private languages of the fourth type, which I will refer to as 'private object' languages.

With these distinctions in mind we can now state the

private language argument as follows, although later on I will mention some variations on this main theme:

(1) A language must have publicly checkable rules.
(2) A private language would not have publicly checkable rules.
(3) Therefore a private language is impossible.

By 'publicly checkable' rules I mean not that the rules are checkable, but that it is possible to check the application of the rule. That is, there must be rules for the use of expressions in a language such that it is possible to tell whether those expressions are being used in accordance with those rules.

The first premiss has attracted most discussion. The point is that words in a language are used according to various implicit rules, and these rules which govern the use of the words give those words their meanings. Moreover, if a word has genuine meaning, if its use is genuinely governed by such rules, then it must be possible to misuse the word, to use it against the rules. A rule which could not be broken would be a very queer rule. If it is possible to misuse the word, to break the rules, then there must be something which establishes whether the word has been misused, whether the rules have been broken. So, it is argued, the rules which govern the use of a word and give that word its meaning must be rules which are publicly checkable, such that it is at least possible for others to tell whether the word has been misused.

But, we might ask, why does this checking have to be public? Why cannot the check for the correct use of the word be a purely private check, capable of being carried out by only the one person? The answer is that if the rule were private and not publicly checkable then there could be no difference between the rule's being kept, the word's being used correctly, and the particular person's merely thinking that it has been kept, that the word has been used correctly. What would decide whether the rule had been kept would simply be whether or not the person thought it had been kept, and, as Wittgenstein puts it (*Philosophical Investigations*, § 202), 'To *think* one is obeying a rule is not to obey a rule.' Suppose, for example, that I say 'I know this is how the word should be used, because I remember that this is how it is used'. Cannot my memory serve as a purely private check as to whether I am using the word correctly? Wittgenstein would say 'No', at least in so far as memory is *all* we have to go on, for there is always the possibility that our memory consistently deceives us: 'Always get rid of the idea of the private object in this way: assume that it constantly changes but that you do not notice the change because your memory constantly deceives you' (p. 207). Memory provides a check only in so far as memory can itself be tested for correctness. 'Justification consists in appealing to something independent' (§ 265).

It is important to realize that Wittgenstein is not saying that memory can never be a test for the correctness of anything. What he is saying is that memory, or anything else for that matter, can be a genuine test for the truth or correctness of something only if it is in turn possible, at least in principle, to check that memory. He gives the example of a man who remembers what time the train goes, and then checks that memory against another memory, his memory of what the timetable looks like. 'If the mental image of the timetable could not itself be *tested* for correctness, how could it confirm the correctness of the first memory? (As if someone were to buy several copies of the morning paper to assure himself that what it said was true)' (§265). The analogy is a little unfair in that checking one memory against another is not like buying different copies of the one paper but rather like buying copies of different papers—and as someone said, 'If it's in the *Daily Telegraph* and the *Morning Star* then it must be true'—but Wittgenstein's point remains. One memory checks another, one newspaper checks another, only in so far as it is possible to establish in turn whether the memories are correct, whether what the papers say is true. So memory cannot be the only test for the correct use of a word; 'justification consists in appealing to something independent'. Surely Wittgenstein is right here: a purely private check, e.g. by means of memory, would not be a genuine check, for there would be no way of telling whether the word was being used correctly and consistently, or whether it only seemed to the person that he was using it correctly and consistently. Which means there would be no way of distinguishing the rule's being kept from its merely seeming to the person that it was being kept. If we are to distinguish a correct use of the word from one which is only apparently correct, there must be some public check which will test the use of the word—and, at the same time, the person's claim to remember how it is used.

So I would accept the first premiss of the private language argument: if a word is to have genuine meaning, if its application is to be genuinely governed by rules, it must be possible to tell when the rules are being kept and when they are not; and so it must be possible to tell when a person is using the word correctly, and when he only thinks that he is using it correctly. Some people have been worried by this, and consequently by the argument which is supposed to follow from it, because it looks suspiciously like the old verification principle in a new form. This, I think, is not so. The verification principle was that a statement has meaning only in so far as it can be verified. The present principle is that a statement has meaning only in so far as it is possible to check the use of the terms used in that statement. We need to distinguish between saying something that is incorrect, false, and using a word incorrectly, misusing it, breaking the rules which govern its use and so determine its meaning. To know the use of a word, in the sense which is of interest to philosophers, is to know what the word is used to say; and to know how to use it is to know to use it when we want to say (assert, ask, command, etc.) various things. There is a difference between knowing how to use it, when to use it, and knowing that to use it on a particular occasion would be to say something true. The fact that I say something false does not necessarily mean that I do not know how to use the expression in question, although it may suggest that I do not. If I say 'It is raining' when it is not this does not necessarily mean that I do not understand, do not know how to use, the word 'raining'. It is even possible to say something which is true and yet be using words incorrectly, as when I say 'It is raining' when it is raining, but meaning to assert that it is cold.[1] What is necessary if a person is to understand what an expression means is not that he be able to tell whether what is said is true, but at most that he know under what conditions it would be true—which is not to say

[1] On what it is to misuse a descriptive term, see Hare, *Freedom and Reason* (Oxford), pp. 8 ff.

that he can tell whether those conditions are satisfied. Matters are confused by the ambiguity of 'I know (or can tell) when p is true'. This might mean 'If p is true I know that it is', or it might mean 'I know what would make p true' (where I may not know whether p is true). What is necessary for understanding p is not being able to tell whether it is true, but at most knowing what would make it true. And the private language argument is not even going this far; it holds only that we must be able to tell whether the expressions are being used correctly.

So the first premiss of the private language argument is not that if a statement is to have genuine meaning we must be able to tell whether it is true, but that if a statement is to have a genuine meaning it must be possible to tell when the words in it are being used correctly, and when they are not. There must be a check not necessarily on the truth of what we say, but on the use of our terms. Even if it is not possible to verify 'There is a God' the statement retains a meaning in so far as it is possible to establish, and check, a consistent use for the terms 'God' and 'exists'. This same point might be made in another way. If language is, in the first place, taught to us by others it must be taught by reference to public phenomena. It is, for example, by reference to such public phenomena as wounds and pain-behaviour that we teach, and learn, and check the use of, the term 'pain'. Thus the first premiss might be stated as that there must be public criteria for the use of a word, there must be criteria by which we can teach the word, learn it, and check that it is being used correctly consistently, according to its agreed meaning, etc.

As well as this premiss there are other similar premisses

leading to the same conclusion. There is, for example, the argument that it is of the nature of a language that it be used for communication, which, together with the premiss that communication is impossible in a private language, yields the conclusion that a private language is impossible. Here too the first premiss seems very plausible, so long as the claim is not that every language must be used for communication—for that would rule out the private codes in which people keep their diaries—but that every language must be capable of being used for communication, and, perhaps, that any language not actually used for communication must be parasitic on one that is.

Again the first premiss might be in the form that a word gets its meaning only from the fact that it has a commonly agreed use, which, together with the premiss that words in a private language will not have a commonly agreed use, yields the conclusion that a private language is impossible. This time the first premiss is supported by the point that a word gets its meaning not from a mere naming ceremony, and in particular not from any form of private christening, but from its use in language and communication. Although my naming some newly discovered bird a 'glump' may lead to 'glump' coming to be the accepted name for the bird, the word 'glump' would not get this meaning just from the fact that I point at the bird and say 'This is a glump'. For if others take no notice of what I say and use some other word as its name, then 'glump' would not mean this particular bird. What would give 'glump' this meaning would be the fact that other people, perhaps following my suggestion, use the word as a name for the bird. As Malcolm puts it (*Knowledge and Certainty*, p. 123):

What makes the . . . sound a *word*, and what makes it the word for *cow*? . . . Is it sufficient that the sound is uttered when and only when a cow is present? Of course not. The sound might refer to anything or nothing. What is necessary is that it should play a part in various activities, in calling, fetching, counting cows, distinguishing cows from other things and pictures of cows from pictures of other things. If the sound has no fixed place in activities ('language-games') of this sort, then it isn't a word for *cow*. To be sure, I can sit in my chair and talk about cows and not be engaged in any of these activities—but what makes my words *refer* to cows is that I have already mastered these activities.

Thus the first premiss of the private language argument has, in its various forms, much to commend it. Those who want to reject the conclusion of the argument spend most of their time attacking these various points when, clearly, we can accept the first premiss and still reject the conclusion, so long as we are prepared to reject the second premiss too. The second premiss deserves more attention than it usually gets. The reason why it does not get much attention is that it seems obvious, even true by definition. Surely a private language is, by definition, one without publicly checkable rules, one which cannot be used for communication, one whose words have no commonly agreed use? But at this point we must remember the distinction between necessarily private languages and private object languages. For it is obviously true that a private language does not have publicly checkable rules, etc., only if by 'private language' we mean a necessarily private language, one which only one person can use and understand. If only one person can understand the language there can be no commonly agreed use for its words, and no communication; whereas if there are publicly checkable rules for the use of those words then it must be possible for others to learn those rules, and so learn the language. Given the first premiss it follows that there cannot be a necessarily private language.

But this is not the conclusion that the private language argument wants, or if it is the conclusion is quite irrelevant to the topic of other minds. The conclusion that people have wanted to draw is not—or at any rate not just—that there cannot be a necessarily private language, but that there cannot be a private object language, a language in which words refer to private objects such as pains are supposed to be (cf. *Philosophical Investigations*, §§ 243–4). The point of Wittgenstein's argument seems to be that, despite appearances, words such as 'pain' do not and cannot name or refer to private objects. In so far as they have any meaning at all (as they surely do) they must have some other function. And, it is suggested, once we see what this other function is the familiar problems about other minds are solved—or rather dissolved, since they cannot even be stated.

Wittgenstein does not deny that pain-sensations occur. ' "But you will surely admit that there is a difference between pain-behaviour accompanied by pain and pain-behaviour without any pain"—Admit it?' Wittgenstein says, 'What greater difference could there be?—"And yet you again and again reach the conclusion that the sensation itself is a nothing"—Not at all. It is not a *something*, but not a *nothing* either! The conclusion was only that a nothing would serve just as well as a something about which nothing could be said' (§ 304). Again: ' "Are you really a behaviourist in disguise? Aren't you at bottom really saying that everything except human behaviour is a fiction?"—If I do speak of a fiction, then it is of a *grammatical* fiction' (§ 307). The point is that private objects cannot be spoken of in a public language, and language must be public, so private objects cannot be spoken of. It follows that words like 'pain' must have some other function than their apparent one of referring to private objects.

2. One's first reaction to all this is to say: But surely English is just such a language, a language where the word 'pain', for example, refers to a private object, a sensation which only the one person is aware of? Now supporters of the argument insist that they are not denying that a word like 'pain' refers to a sensation (cf. Malcolm, *Knowledge and Certainty*, p. 121). Obviously to talk about a man's pains is to talk about his sensations. Nevertheless, the argument runs, we should not think that when we talk about a man's sensations we are referring to something which is private to him, something which he alone is aware of. This is what is held to be impossible when it is held that a private object language is impossible. We think that a private object language is possible, and that English is just such a language, because we make the mistake of construing words like 'pain' on what Wittgenstein calls the model of object and name; we make the mistake of thinking that 'pain' refers to an object, the sensation, in just the way that, for example, 'table' refers to an object, the thing I am writing on. But in fact 'pain', and similar words, do not function in this way.

Thus the claim is that 'Jones has a pain in the middle of his chest' is not like 'Jones has a nose in the middle of his face'. Since only Jones can feel what is in his chest, the word 'pain' cannot refer to what is in the middle of his chest in the way that the word 'nose' does refer to what is in the middle of his face. What, then, does the word 'pain' refer to? Since it is because of his behaviour, including what he says, that we say that Jones has the pain, it is tempting to say that 'pain' must refer to his behaviour, and so conclude that Wittgenstein is, in spite of all, a behaviourist. But Wittgenstein would insist that to say that Jones feels a pain is not just to say that he does and says various things; it is also to react to Jones in a certain way, in the way that people react to their fellows when they feel pains. To say that Jones feels a pain is to take up an attitude towards him, it is to think of him as in need of sympathy, pity, analgesic, and so on. As Malcolm puts it (*Knowledge and Certainty*, p. 118).

In the *Investigations*, Wittgenstein says 'My attitude towards him is an attitude towards a soul. I am not of the *opinion* that he has a soul' (p. 178). I do not *believe* that the man is suffering who writhes before me—for to what facts would a 'belief' be related, such that a change in the facts would lead me to alter it. I *react* to his suffering. I look at him with compassion and try to comfort him. . . . The thought that behind someone's pain-behaviour is the pain itself does not enter into our use of 'He's in pain', but what does enter into it is our sympathetic, or unsympathetic, reaction to him. The fact that the latter does enter into our use of that sentence (but might not have) gives sense to saying that the sentence 'He is in pain' does not just *mean* that his behaviour and circumstances are such and such—although these are the criteria for its use.

The idea is, then, that the difference between 'He feels a pain' and 'He is bleeding, groaning, wincing, etc.' is not that the former involves the claim that behind the pain-behaviour is the pain itself and the latter does not, but that the former involves our taking up various attitudes, having various feelings, towards the person in question. But surely precisely the same is true of 'He is bleeding, groaning, wincing'. As Wittgenstein himself would insist, we find it difficult if not impossible not to take up these attitudes towards someone who is bleeding, groaning, wincing, so this reference to attitudes and feelings cannot bring out a difference between 'He feels a pain' and 'He is bleeding, groaning, wincing' after all!

Perhaps Malcolm would say that although we would naturally adopt these attitudes towards anyone who was bleeding, groaning, wincing, saying that he is bleeding, groaning, wincing does not *necessarily involve* our taking up these attitudes in the way that saying he feels a pain does. Or more accurately—since we can, in a sense, say anything —believing that someone feels a pain necessarily involves taking up these attitudes towards him, in a way that believing merely that he bleeds, groans, winces, does not. That is, it is possible, at least in principle, to believe that he bleeds, groans, winces, and yet not feel towards him in the way that we feel towards those who feel pains. But it is not possible, even in principle, to believe that he feels a pain, and yet not feel towards him in this way.

But what are these attitudes? It is quite possible to believe that someone feels a pain and yet not to care about it at all, even to be quite glad. Malcolm may say that even this is to take up an attitude, albeit an unsympathetic one, of the sort we take towards people who feel pains, but now his position collapses into triviality. If even indifference counts as such an attitude, then the claim that believing that he feels a pain necessarily involves our taking up some attitude towards him amounts merely to the claim that we will feel something towards him or we will not, as the case may be. The argument is that there are certain attitudes which we have to have towards Jones if we are to believe that he feels a pain, as opposed to believing merely that he bleeds, groans, winces, but there are no particular attitudes which we have to have. We may be glad, or sorry, or indifferent. Of course, if not caring twopence either way counts as having an attitude then it will be true, necessarily and trivially, that when we believe he feels a pain we have some attitude towards him, but precisely the same holds true when we believe that he is bleeding, groaning, wincing. Malcolm has still failed to explain the difference between saying that a man feels a pain and saying that he bleeds, groans, winces, etc.

Ordinarily we would want to say that the difference consists not in any attitudes we take—since we will very likely take the same attitudes in either case—but in the fact that 'He feels a pain' refers to, mentions, something which 'He is bleeding, groaning, wincing' does not, viz. the sensation which 'lies behind' and is responsible for the groaning and wincing. This is what Malcolm wishes to deny, but his failure to provide an alternative explanation of the difference can only reflect back on the argument that leads him to the denial. Moreover, even if Malcolm's suggestion about the function of 'He feels a pain' were acceptable, there would still be scope for the other minds scepticism we have been discussing. The sceptic insists that we cannot prove that, for example, when people display pain-behaviour they are feeling pains. This seems correct so long as it is possible for people to exhibit pain-behaviour and yet not feel pains. The point of the private language argument seems to be that this is not possible, that although not self-contradictory the sceptic's point is incoherent in that what he tries to say cannot be said. We cannot refer to pains in the way the sceptic tries to. Now Malcolm suggests that to say that a person feels a pain is to say that he acts, or is inclined to act, in various ways, and also to take up certain attitudes towards him. If this is so then presumably the sceptic's suggestion that there might, in principle, be pain-behaviour but no pains is equivalent to the suggestion that we might, in principle, observe people's pain-behaviour and yet not take up the appropriate attitudes towards them. Clearly this is possible, at least in principle, so even on Malcolm's interpretation the suggestion that there might be pain-behaviour but no pains is perfectly coherent.

So far we have concentrated on the third-person 'He feels a pain'. The difficulties are, if anything, worse when we turn to first-person statements like 'I feel a pain' or 'I am thinking about the Budget'. The natural interpretation of 'I feel a pain in my finger' is that I am reporting the existence of something, a sensation, which I alone am aware of. If I am not doing this, what am I doing? The suggestion—what for Wittgenstein (§ 244) was but one possibility—is that saying 'I feel a pain' is no more than a sophisticated piece of pain-behaviour. Now clearly there is no point in denying that 'I feel a pain' (or more naturally 'It hurts') may, like 'Ouch' or a groan, be an expression of pain, just as 'I love you' may, like a sigh or a blush, be an expression of love. But 'I feel a pain' and 'I love you' are also reports, and are far more like other statements than they are like groans or sighs. At first Malcolm credited Wittgenstein with discovering 'the arresting fact that my sentences about my present sensations have

[margin, handwritten] Surely wrong; what about 'I had a pain yesterday' are we feeling pain now & what we are saying that.

the same logical status as my outcries and facial expressions' (p. 111), but later he realized that this is not a fact at all. 'By saying the sentence one can make a *statement*; it has a *contradictory*; it is *true* or *false*; in saying it one *lies* or *tells the truth*; and so on. None of these things, exactly, can be said of crying, limping, holding one's leg' (p. 140). This shows quite clearly that 'I feel a pain' has the logical status of a report or an assertion.

An equally damaging objection is that the suggestion works for only a very small minority of first-person psychological statements. 'I feel a pain' might be used as an expression of pain rather than as a report or a description, but what are we to make of 'I felt a pain yesterday' (delayed pain-behaviour perhaps?), 'If I feel a pain I'll go and see the doctor' (hypothetical pain-behaviour perhaps?), 'I don't feel a pain' (non-pain-behaviour perhaps?). And what could 'I am thinking about the Budget' or 'I see it clearly in my mind's eye' be expressions of? What are the 'natural, non-verbal, behavioural expressions of psychological states' (p. 140) that these are to be assimilated to? The theory cannot even begin to work for them.

All of this is quite enough to show that 'I feel a pain' is a report, an assertion, and not merely a piece of pain-behaviour like a cry or a groan. The only question is why anyone should ever have thought otherwise. Malcolm has mentioned two things which, he thinks, give a point to comparing 'I feel a pain' with a cry or a groan.

First of all (*Knowledge and Certainty*, p. 110) there is the point that we cannot be mistaken in saying 'I feel a pain' just as we cannot be mistaken in groaning. I would be prepared to argue that this is simply false—children, for example, sometimes think they are hurt when they are not. But even if it were true, the differences between 'I feel a pain' and groaning would still be more important than the similarities. The former would be incorrigible in that it could not be false without my knowing that it was, whereas the latter is incorrigible in that the true-false distinction does not apply at all.

But perhaps Malcolm would not accept that there is this difference. He wants to say that we cannot identify or recognize (and hence cannot mis-identify or 'mis-recognize') such things as feeling pains. 'A man cannot be in *error* as to whether he is in pain. . . . It is senseless to suppose that he has wrongly identified a tickle as a pain' (p. 110). Personally I can see no grounds at all for the claim that we cannot identify or recognize our own sensations. In fact this must be possible even on Malcolm's own theory. Saying 'I feel a pain' is supposed to be a piece of learnt pain-behaviour, so we have to learn when that behaviour is appropriate and when it is not. To do that we have to learn to recognize or identify our present state as being one of the kind for which saying 'I feel a pain' is an appropriate piece of behaviour. That is, before I can learn this sophisticated piece of pain-behaviour I must be able to identify the state of which it is to be an expression. I think Malcolm's mistake must have been a misreading of Wittgenstein's point about the use of memory as a check for correctness. As we saw (p. 75 above), the point is that memory, or anything else for that matter, cannot show us that a certain belief is correct unless there is, at least in principle, some independent way of checking the correctness of that memory. Wittgenstein does not say that memory can never check the correctness of anything. So although Malcolm may be right to say (p. 140) that we do not and cannot identify pains by comparing the sensation to some inner paradigm, we can and do use our memories to recognize and identify what we feel. I know that this, that I feel, is a pain because I know (remember) that sensations like this go with wounds and groans, and because I know (remember) that such sensations are called 'pains'.

Part of the trouble is that the question 'How do we identify pains?' is ambiguous.[1] If it means 'How do we tell that this is a pain?' then, clearly, memory can have a role to play, so long as there is some way of checking that my memory, my recognition, is correct—which there is, for example, by kicking me in the spot I claim hurts, and seeing whether I scream. But if the question means 'What makes this sensation *a pain*?' then what counts is not anyone's memory, but the fact that the sensation is linked with wounds and pain-behaviour. My memory may tell me that this is the smell of onions, but it isn't my memory that makes it the smell of onions. We will see in the next section that it is its connexion with pain-behaviour that establishes, determines, that a certain sensation is a pain sensation. But this does not mean that the only way to tell that it is a pain is by observing the pain-behaviour. It is the fact that he is crowned in Westminster Abbey which establishes, determines, that this man is King of England, but that does not mean that the only way to tell that he is King of England is by observing his Coronation. Just as I can recognize what I smell as the smell of onions, without having to check that it comes from onions, so I can recognize what I feel as a pain, without having to

[1] We will have more to say about this ambiguity in Chapter VII, Section 4.

check that it makes me wince, even though it is, in the end, my tendency to wince that marks the sensation as a pain sensation, and not, say, a kinaesthetic sensation.

Malcolm's second reason (pp. 139-40) for likening 'I feel a pain' to a groan or a cry is that once we notice the similarities between the two we will no longer want to ask the absurd question 'How does one know when to say "I feel a pain"?' (cf. 'How does one know when to groan?'). It is difficult to see what Malcolm is getting at here. Personally I feel no temptation to ask 'How does one know when to say "I feel a pain"?', just as I feel no temptation to ask 'How does one know when to say "I am married"?' There are two questions which I might want to ask, but neither of them is absurd. I might want to ask 'How does one know whether "I feel a pain", said by oneself, is true?' The answer is 'From what you feel'. Or I might want to ask 'How does one learn to say "I feel a pain", and not "Pirots Karulize elatically" when one is in pain?' This is a straightforward question about language-learning, and has an answer even if 'I feel a pain' is no more than a piece of pain-behaviour. In actual fact this brings out a difference, not a similarity, between saying 'I feel a pain' and groaning, in that we have to learn to say 'My leg hurts' as we do not have to learn to cry, limp, or hold our leg.

Malcolm gets into all these difficulties because he is particularly concerned to reject the traditional view, which may underlie the argument from analogy, that it is only 'from one's own case' that one can know what, for example, pain is. In one way this traditional view is clearly wrong, but in another it is clearly right. It is only from your own case that you know what pain is *like*; if I have never had migraine then I do not know what it is like to have migraine. But even if I have never had it, I can and do know what people are talking about when they talk about migraine, I know what 'migraine' means. The Oxfam advertisement 'You know the word malnutrition, he knows what it means' plays upon an ambiguity in 'means'. A philosopher might prefer to say 'You know what "malnutrition" means, he knows what it is'. However, Malcolm is quite right to insist that it isn't my feeling toothache that tells me what the word means. I know what 'tooth-ache' means not because I feel it, but because I have observed and learnt how other people use this word, how in various situations they ascribe it to themselves, to each other, and to me. It is in the same way that I come to know what 'migraine' means, even if I never suffer from it myself.

Thus I learn what 'pain' means, and therefore in that sense what pain is, by seeing how, on what criteria, people use the word. These criteria are of course behavioural. Yet when I ascribe pain to myself, when I say 'I feel a pain', I do not do this on the basis of behavioural criteria. Indeed I do not seem to use any criteria at all. This is why Malcolm rejects as absurd the question 'How does one know when to say "I feel a pain"?', and the conclusion is drawn that when I say 'I feel a pain' I cannot be asserting or reporting anything at all. This is simply a response that I have learned to make, as the Englishman but not the Russian learns to say 'Ouch' when someone stands on his toe, a response to which other people react as they react to my groans and cries.

Now Malcolm is clearly right to say that I do not have to tell that I feel a pain. I may have to tell, or at any rate remember, that it is (called) a pain, but I do not have to tell that

I feel it; we saw in Chapter II that it is simply a fact of logic that if you think, perceive, or feel a pain, then you know that you do. Malcolm puts this by saying that I 'have no criterion' for saying 'I feel a pain', and this seems to be his reason for denying that 'I feel a pain' is an assertion or report. It may also be his reason for denying that we can recognize or identify what we feel as a pain. Certainly if it were true that there is no way of knowing, learning, when it is correct to use the expression 'I feel a pain', then that would be a good reason for denying that it embodies a genuine assertion. Again, if it were true that there is nothing which justifies me in saying, nothing which makes it true for me to say, 'I feel a pain', then that would be a good reason for denying that it embodies a genuine assertion. But neither of these things is true. One 'lacks a criterion' for saying 'I feel a pain' only in the sense that there is nothing that tells me that I feel a pain. To say that this shows that 'I feel a pain' is not a genuine assertion is to opt for verificationism in its most extreme form: an expression is not a genuine assertion unless I have some way of telling that it is true or false. Not that I think Malcolm means to adopt verificationism although the reasoning on p. 139 of *Knowledge and Certainty* seems to be that since 'I feel a pain' does not report a (self-)observation, it cannot report anything at all! Rather his mistake is to confuse the claim that we have no way of telling when we feel pains, with the claim that there is no way of learning when, under what circumstances it would be correct, to say 'I feel a pain'. If the latter were correct then it would justify his conclusion that 'I feel a pain' cannot be an assertion, but it is not correct. The former is correct, but it does not justify Malcolm's conclusion.

3. Thus the conclusion of the private language argument—
that a word like 'pain' does not and cannot name, refer to,
a private object, something which only the one person is
aware of—is grossly implausible. We have yet to look at
the argument which is supposed to establish this conclusion,
for all that has been shown so far is that a necessarily private
language is impossible. What is still to be shown is that a
private object language is impossible.

There are two ways in which we might try to establish
this further conclusion. First it might be argued that our
distinction between a necessarily private and a private object
language is not a genuine, or at least not a relevant, distinction, in that any private object language will be a necessarily
private language and, as such, impossible. Or it might be
argued that private object languages, like necessarily private
languages, will not have publicly checkable rules for the use
of their terms, and will therefore, by the previous argument,
be impossible. Let us begin with the first of these moves.

Will a private object language also be a necessarily private
language? Is it the case that a language which referred to
private objects would be understandable by only one person,
the person who is aware of those objects? Most supporters
of the private language argument seem to have simply taken
it for granted that this is so, without making it clear why
they think that it is (e.g. Wittgenstein, *Philosophical
Investigations*, § 243; Malcolm, *Knowledge and Certainty*, p. 97).
Perhaps part of the reason is a simple failure to distinguish
the two types of private language, but there is another factor
at work here: the verification principle. Once we agree that
the meaning of a word is determined by the method, or the
possibility, of verification of sentences containing that word,

and also agree that it is in some sense impossible to verify whether or not some other person feels a private sensation such as a pain, then it follows that a sentence like 'He feels a pain' can have no meaning. Given the verification theory, talk about pains and the like will have meaning only for those who can verify the existence of those pains, i.e. those who feel the pains, and so a private object language will be a necessarily private language. Or perhaps, since the conclusion that a sentence like 'He feels a pain' is meaningless is clearly absurd, those who adopt a verification theory of meaning will want to find some other interpretation of this sentence, some interpretation which enables them to say that the sentence has meaning even for those who do not feel the sensation. This, of course, is precisely what supporters of the private language argument try to do.

Nevertheless it is clear that a simple appeal to the verification theory of meaning is not going to carry much weight. If the private language argument depends simply on the verification theory then we can agree with Mrs. Thompson ('Private Languages', *American Philosophical Quarterly*, 1964, p. 30): 'Whatever can be said both for and against the one can be said both for and against the other. The only trouble is: The arguments on both sides are excessively familiar.' Even so we should not conclude, as Mrs. Thompson does, that the private language argument is just a new application of the old verification theory, for that would be to forget the second way of turning the original argument into an argument against private object languages. Indeed, although I have found her paper very helpful, I cannot accept Mrs. Thompson's formulation of the private language argument. She holds that the argument is based on the principle 'A sign "K" is not a kind-name in a man's language unless it is possible to find out whether or not a thing is K' (p. 29), and she does not so much refute this principle as say 'Take it or leave it—it's the verification principle again.' But first of all I do not see how this principle, even if accepted, is supposed to establish the desired conclusion, which she states as 'There can be no such thing as a language in which it is logically impossible that anyone else but its speaker should have any good reason at all for thinking he under-understands.' I fear that Mrs. Thompson is at one with those supporters of the argument who fail to distinguish between a necessarily private language, which is what is denied by the conclusion as she states it, and a private object language, which is supposed to be ruled out by the principle that she states. Moreover, I doubt whether this principle is an accurate summary of the argument, or, for that matter, whether it is equivalent to the verification principle. The argument is, as we have seen, that a word cannot be being used according to proper rules, as is necessary if the word is to have a genuine meaning, unless it is possible to tell whether a person is using that word according to the rules, as opposed to merely thinking that he is using it correctly. Now to say that it must be possible to tell whether a word is being used correctly is not to insist, as the verificationists did, that a sentence cannot make sense unless we can tell whether it is true or false. We have seen (p. 77 above) that there is a distinction, which Mrs. Thompson is once more at one with the supporters of the argument in not noticing, between saying that we must be able to tell that the word is being used correctly, and saying that we must be able to tell whether what is said is true.

We now turn to the second method of turning the original argument into an argument against the possibility of private object languages, the argument that they, like necessarily private languages, are impossible because they would be languages without publicly checkable rules. The argument seems to be that if a word were to refer to something which only the one person could be aware of, then only that person could know whether the word was being used correctly. If that were so the rules governing the use of the word, the rules which lay it down when the word is being used correctly and when it is not, would not be publicly checkable. The only test for whether the word was being used correctly would be the particular person's memory of how it should be used. To repeat: 'Always get rid of the idea of the private object in this way: assume that it constantly changes, but that you do not notice the change because your memory constantly deceives you' (*Philosophical Investigations*, p. 207).

It seems to me that this argument depends on the ambiguity, or at least lack of clarity, in talk of a word's being used correctly or incorrectly. We have seen that there is a difference between a word's being used correctly or incorrectly, in accordance with the rules governing its use and determining its meaning, and a word's being used to say something true or false. When people claim that we cannot tell whether another feels a pain this does nothing to show that we cannot tell how to use the word 'pain', nor that the rules governing the use of that word, and so determining its meaning, are not publicly checkable. Even if we cannot tell when another feels a pain, 'pain' will be a genuine word with a genuine meaning so long as there are publicly checkable rules which determine when it is and when it is not correct to call something a pain. The question is whether the fact that a word refers to a private object means that the rules which govern its use, and so determine its meaning, cannot be publicly checkable. This does not seem to me to be so. A name gets its meaning from the thing, or rather the sort of thing, it names, i.e. to give the meaning of a name is to explain what sort or sorts of thing it is the name of. The rules which govern the meaning of a name will be rules which state what a thing has to be like before it can correctly be called by that name. Given the earlier argument about the need that these rules be publicly checkable, this means that it must be possible for people in general to tell when a thing is of that kind, whether it possesses such features as make it correct to call it by that name. So in so far as 'pain' is a name, as it seems to be, it must be possible for people in general to tell when something is a pain, when it is correct to refer to some item as 'a pain'. As Wittgenstein says (§ 580), 'An "inner process" stands in need of outward criteria.' So if we are to know what pains are, if this word is to have any meaning at all for us, there must be public ways of telling when something is a pain and when it is not. Whether or not it is possible to tell whether pains other than our own exist, the fact is that there are public ways of telling when something, given that it exists, is a pain. How do I know that this, which I feel, is a pain? Because it feels like one. How do I know that sensations which feel like this are pains? Because they are sensations of the sort I get when I am wounded, which make me want to cry out, etc. This, then, is what we mean by a pain: a sensation of the sort we get when we are wounded, of the sort that makes us want to cry and clutch the wounded part of our body, etc. My elders and betters taught me what 'pain' meant even though they did not and could not know how my sensations felt because they did not and could not feel them. It was by reference to my wounds and injuries and pain-behaviour that they taught me what 'pain' means, what sort of thing it is the name of. They taught me that 'pain' is the name for the sensation that goes with injuries and pain-behaviour. Wounds, pain-behaviour, and the like provide the public, outward criteria by which we determine whether or not a sensation is a pain sensation.

There are, then, publicly checkable rules which govern the application and thus the meaning of 'pain'. If a person sincerely asserts that he feels a pain when in fact he is laughing, smiling, and showing no signs of strain or injury then we know that he is misusing the word 'pain'. There are public rules which lay down when it is correct to call a sensation a pain sensation, and so it is always possible, at least in principle, for people to tell whether something is a pain sensation. But this does not mean that it is always possible, even in principle, for people to tell whether such an item *exists*, whether a person does feel the sensation in question. For the argument was only that those rules which govern the use of a word and so determine its meaning must be publicly checkable, and the rule that a sensation must exist if we are to say of someone that he feels a pain is not a rule which governs the use of 'pain' in the sense of determining its meaning. To say that someone feels a pain when no sensation exists, is felt, is to say something that is false, but it is not to use 'pain' contrary to its meaning. It is not part of the meaning of 'pain' that such sensations, or any

sensations at all, exist; indeed it is pretty much of a philosophical commonplace that the meaning of a term cannot
determine whether the thing in question exists. The rule 'For
a person to feel a pain a sensation must exist' is not a rule
determining the meaning of 'pain', but a rule determining
when it is true to say of someone that he feels a pain. The
argument for the need for publicly checkable rules governing the use and meaning of 'pain' does not seem to count at
all against other minds scepticism.

Where, then, has the private language argument gone
wrong? Let us look at it again: the conclusion is that there
cannot be a private object language, a language in which
words refer to private objects. And the reason for this conclusion is that words must have publicly checkable rules for
their use, that words cannot have private meanings. But
there is, of course, a difference between meaning and reference, so the fact that a word has a private reference does not
mean that it has to have a private meaning; there is no reason
why a word should not refer to a private object and yet have
a meaning that is publicly ascertainable and publicly checkable. It seems that the private language argument in its
present form depends not so much on the verification theory
of meaning as on an even older error: the failure to distinguish between meaning and reference. Thus Wittgenstein, for example, says (§ 243): 'The individual words of
this language are to refer to what can only be known to the
person speaking; to his immediate private sensations. So
another person cannot understand the language.' He as-
sumes, without argument, that if only the speaker can know
what the word *refers* to only the speaker can know what it
means. And this is clearly false; even if I am the only one

who is acquainted with the pain it does not follow that I am the only one who understands 'There is a pain in my toe'. An even more obvious indication of this mistake is to be found in Strawson's exposition of Wittgenstein's argument, in his review of the *Philosophical Investigations* (*Mind*, 1954, p. 84). Strawson distinguishes a strong and a weak thesis which Wittgenstein may have held, the weak thesis being that public criteria are necessary for the ascription of sensation words, and the strong thesis being that no words name sensations. And, adds Strawson, the weak thesis leads to the strong thesis if we say, as many including myself would want to say, that the meaning of a word consists, in some way, in the criteria for its application. But *this* does not turn the weak thesis into the strong. What would do that would be the claim that the criteria for the application of a word are the same as the reference of the word, and this seems obviously wrong. Thus we can accept the weak thesis, and the identification of meaning and criteria, and still reject the strong thesis, that no words name or refer to private sensations.

To sum up, my positive conclusions are:

(1) A necessarily private language is impossible.
(2) The use of a word must be governed by publicly checkable rules, rules whose satisfaction is publicly checkable, so that we can (*a*) check whether the word is being used correctly, and (*b*) teach its meaning— and for that matter its reference—to other people.
(3) Consequently 'pain' means 'a sensation of a certain sort', where the sort in question is determined not by how it feels, but by its causes and effects and the

behaviour which characteristically accompanies it. A sensation's being a pain sensation is not a matter of how it feels, but a matter of its being of the sort caused by bodily damage and leading to pain-behaviour. Similarly a sensation's being a sensation of cold is not a matter of how it feels, but a matter of its being a sensation of the sort caused by frost and snow and leading to shivering, etc. And similarly for other sensations.

In all of this I follow Wittgenstein, but I reject his further claim that a private object language is impossible, that words cannot refer to private sensations. I have argued that this further claim is a result of making any or all of the following mistakes:

(1) Failing to distinguish private object languages from necessarily private languages.

(2) Adopting a verification theory of meaning, with its consequence that if we cannot verify the existence of a private object such as a pain any word allegedly referring to such a private object can have no meaning.

(3) Confusing meaning with reference, at least to the extent of thinking that if a word has a private object for its reference then its meaning, and the criteria for its application which govern that meaning, will have to be private also.

4. We have yet to discover the full explanation of how Wittgenstein and others come to make this grossly implausible claim that words cannot refer to private objects, sensations of which only the one person is aware. A very important

point is that in his discussion Wittgenstein does not distinguish the claim that pains and the like are things which only the one person can feel, from the claim that pains and the like are things which only the one person can know. I have defined a private object as something which only the one person can be aware of, but there are at least two ways in which we talk of people being aware of things. We talk about a person being aware of, i.e. perceiving, some item, as when we say that he is aware of some sound or smell or pain. And we talk about a person being aware of, i.e. realizing, some fact, as when we say that he is aware that two and two make four, that vivisection hurts the animal, that he has made a fool of himself. When I defined a private object as one which only the one person can be aware of I meant awareness in the sense of perception—a pain is a private object inasmuch as a pain is something which only one person can feel. I did not mean that pains are private objects in the sense that only the one person can know of their existence. That is simply false.

But suppose we do take 'private object' to mean 'something which only the one person can know of'. Can there be a private object language in this sense of 'private object', a language in which terms refer to things which only the one person can have knowledge of? It seems clear that there cannot, for such a language would be a necessarily private language, and we have seen that such languages are impossible. That is, if I am the only one who can know anything about x then I am the only one who can know what 'x' means, and consequently 'x' cannot be a genuine term in my, or any, language. Thus the private language argument does provide a refutation for the scepticism which asserts that I alone can know that I feel a pain. 'In one way this is false, and in another nonsense' (§ 246).

So Wittgenstein succeeds in his main purpose, which is to show that the claim that only I can know whether I am really in pain cannot be correct, that it is either false or incoherent. But his mistake is to think that this absurd scepticism follows from a certain theory of language, a certain interpretation of the function of words like 'pain', a theory which must therefore be mistaken. Wittgenstein does not argue both that the scepticism is absurd because it is based on a mistaken theory of language, and that the theory of language is mistaken because it leads to an absurd scepticism. Rather he argues that the sceptical conclusion is absurd, and therefore that the theory of language which commits us to it must be mistaken. But Wittgenstein is himself mistaken in thinking that it is the theory of language which commits us to scepticism about other minds.

The absurdity of 'Only I can know whether I feel a pain' is supposed to show that words like 'pain' cannot refer to private objects, sensations which only the one person can feel. But of course it does not follow from the claim that 'pain' refers to a private sensation that others cannot know that I am feeling a pain. The fact that I am referring to something I alone feel does not mean that you cannot know whether what I say is true, much less that you cannot know what I am saying, what I am talking about. This follows only if we add the extra premiss that what I alone can feel, I alone can have knowledge of. It is this extra premiss that leads to scepticism, and it is this extra premiss which is mistaken. It is tantamount to the claim that only eyewitnesses can have knowledge of what happens! The fact that I am the only one who feels the pain does not mean that I am the only one who can know that I feel a pain, and there is therefore no need to think that 'pain' cannot refer to something which I alone feel.

In fact we can now see that Wittgenstein makes precisely the same mistake as the sceptic. The argument is: if 'pain' did refer to a private sensation then only the one person could know that he feels a pain; we can and do know that others feel pains; therefore 'pain' cannot refer to a private sensation. But the first premiss is simply false. Wittgenstein does not notice that this—and not a mistake about language—is the mistake that the sceptic makes.

All of this comes out clearly when we consider the celebrated example of the beetle in the box:

Now suppose someone tells me that *he* knows what pain is only from his own case!—Suppose everyone had a box with something in it: we call it a 'beetle'. No one can look into anyone else's box, and everyone says he knows what a beetle is only by looking at *his* beetle.—Here it would be quite possible for everyone to have something different in his box. One might even imagine such a thing constantly changing.—But suppose the word 'beetle' had a use in these people's language?—If so it would not be used as the name of a thing. The thing in the box has no place in the language-game at all; not even as a *something*: for the box might even be empty.—No, one can 'divide through' by the thing in the box; it cancels out, whatever it is. That is to say: if we construe the grammar of the expression of sensation on the model of 'object and name' the object drops out of consideration as irrelevant (293).

Wittgenstein is saying that if the word 'beetle' is to have a use in these people's language it cannot be used as the name of a thing, the thing in the box which only the one person can see. Similarly if the word 'pain' is to have a use in our language, as surely it has, it cannot be used as the name of a thing, a sensation which only the one person can feel. But consider what use 'beetle' would have for these people—and similarly what use 'pain' has for us. The word gets its meaning from its use, and since these people use 'beetle' to talk about what is in their boxes, 'beetle' will mean 'that which is in the box'. This meaning is established by the agreed use of the term, and it is possible for anyone to check whether the word is being used correctly, viz. to talk about what is in the box. The rules for the use of the word are publicly checkable. But some one might think that since the word is used to talk about what is in his box, the word 'beetle' must be the name for the thing, or the type of thing, that he finds in his box. Suppose I call the thing in my box 'Ringo' I might think that 'beetle' means 'things like Ringo', just as 'table' means 'things like the object I am writing on'. But 'beetle' cannot mean that, because if it did it would be impossible to tell, when others spoke of their beetles, whether they were using the word correctly or not. If 'beetle' meant 'thing like Ringo', and you said 'There is a beetle in my box', you would be saying 'There is a thing like Ringo in my box'. So since it is impossible for me or for you to tell whether the thing in your box is like Ringo—only you can see what is in your box, and only I can see Ringo—we could not tell whether the word was being used correctly. All that 'beetle' can mean, for the people in the example, is 'the thing in the box, whatever it is'. Even if the things in the different boxes were all different they would still all be beetles, because what makes them beetles is just the fact that they are in the boxes. We could not even ask whether one beetle was like another, whether what is in my box is like what is in yours, because we could not say what one beetle was like in itself. The moment we try to describe what I alone can see we will be using words in a way which is not publicly check-able, and therefore not really using words, not using real words, at all.

Now Wittgenstein says that the people in his example could not use 'beetle' as the name of a thing. This is true in a sense, but only in a sense. 'Beetle' could not be used to mean, for example, 'thing like the one, called Ringo, in my box'; in that sense 'beetle' could not be the name of what is in the box. But in another sense it is the name of the thing in the box; as Wittgenstein himself says, we call the thing in the box a 'beetle'. The point is, as we saw, that 'beetle' is not the name of a particular thing in a particular box, but rather the name for what is in any box, whatever it may be. 'Beetle' means 'that which is in the box, whatever it is like'. The same will be true of 'pain'; by 'pain' we mean 'the thing we feel when we are wounded, which makes us want to cry out, etc., whatever that sensation may be like'. Even if what you feel when you are wounded is not at all like what I feel when I am wounded, what you and I feel are both pains, just as even if what is in your box is quite different from what is in my box they are both beetles. Because 'beetle' means 'whatever is in the box' and 'pain' means 'whatever it is that we feel in such and such circumstances'.

Now if this is so, and I am sure that it is, we have used Wittgenstein's example to draw a very unWittgensteinean conclusion. For his argument was that words cannot name private objects, and we have just concluded that 'pain' does name a private object, the sensation, whatever it may be like, we feel in certain circumstances. The reason why 'beetle' could not be the name of a thing was, apparently, that the thing might be a nothing, the box might be empty, which means that the thing is irrelevant to the use of the word. Yet is the existence of the thing referred to *ever* relevant to the use, the meaning, of a name? We can talk about what does not exist, so a word can have meaning even if the thing in question does not exist. More than that, it can still refer, be a name, even if the thing in question does not exist. The mere fact that the box might be empty does not mean that 'beetle' cannot be a name for the thing in the box; it means only that the reference might be unsuccessful. Presumably what Wittgenstein meant was that 'beetle' cannot refer to what is in the box unless we can *tell* whether the reference succeeds or fails. But what is the justification of this requirement? It looks like the verification principle again—if we cannot tell whether the universe began in some primordial cosmic explosion does this mean that 'primordial cosmic explosion' cannot refer to the explosion, even if there was one? What is necessary if 'beetle' is to be the name of, refer to, the thing in the box is not that we be able to tell whether the reference succeeds, but that we be able to tell that this is how the word is being used, viz. to refer to the thing in the box. What is necessary is that the word have a public meaning, not that it have a public reference.

But this confusion of meaning and reference is not Wittgenstein's only mistake, nor for our present purposes the most important mistake. For it is just plain false to say that we cannot tell whether the reference succeeds or fails, whether or not there is a thing in the box. Presumably the people in the example know what it is for one thing to be inside another, so if a person has nothing in his box he will tell us. When told to look at his beetle he will naturally retort 'But there isn't anything in my box'. Similarly if a person did not feel pain, then when he is told that by pain we mean not his behaviour nor what he says nor the part of his body where we have kicked him, he will naturally retort 'But there isn't anything over and above these—I am not aware of any pain.' This will tell us that he does not feel a pain. If we construe the grammar of the expression of sensation on the model of 'object and name' the object drops out as irrelevant only in that it does not matter what the object is like 'in itself'. It does matter that some object exist. Of course you might say that appealing to what a person says and does, does not, in the last resort, prove that there is a beetle in his box, a pain in his toe, but this is to agree with the sceptic, not to refute him. The main point is that the fact that only I can see the beetle in my box does not necessarily mean that only I can know that there is one there, just as the fact that only I can feel the pain in my toe does not necessarily mean that only I can know that there is one there.

We can now see that Wittgenstein's argument that 'beetle', and similarly 'pain', cannot function as the name of a thing rests on the assumption that if a term did have a private reference then only that one person could know whether what was said was true, that if 'pain' did refer to a private sensation only I could know whether I feel a pain. This is the very assumption that leads to scepticism, and this is the assumption that is mistaken. Wittgenstein fails to see that this assumption is involved in his own argument as much as in the sceptic's, partly because of his basic desire to show that all philosophical errors arise from a misunderstanding of the workings of language, and partly because he does not distinguish the claim that pains and the like are things which only one person can feel from the claim that they are things which only one person can know. We have only to notice this distinction to realize that the latter does not follow from the former, just as it does not follow from the fact that I alone can hear the dog-whistle that I alone can know that it is sounding. You can know that it is sounding, either because you see it being blown or because I tell you that it is. Similarly you can know that I feel a pain, either because you see me wince or because I tell you that I feel it.

CHAPTER VI

The Argument from Criteria

1. EARLIER (p. 59 above) I quoted a passage from Sidney Shoemaker in which he argued that there must be some non-contingent, conceptual connexion between physical states and psychological states if we are ever to have knowledge of the latter. In itself this point is not likely to worry the sceptic, since he is quite content to conclude that we do not have knowledge of other minds. But the point would carry more weight if it were argued that unless there is some non-contingent, conceptual connexion between the two it would be impossible to make sense of any claim about the psychological states of others. For if it is impossible to make sense of the claim, for example, that another feels a pain, it must also be impossible to make sense of the claim that we know that he does, and hence impossible to make sense of the sceptic's claim that we do not know whether he does. This is an argument which is suggested by the writings of Norman Malcolm, I will call it 'the argument from criteria'.

It runs as follows: If an expression is to have a sense there must be criteria governing its use and application, criteria whose satisfaction establishes beyond question that the expression is being used and applied correctly. If 'He feels a pain' or 'He is thinking about the Budget' are to have a sense there must be criteria which establish when these expressions are being used correctly. So the sceptic who claims that there is no way of telling is caught in a dilemma

If there is no way of telling, no criterion, then the expression 'He feels a pain', and also the expression 'There is no way of telling whether he feels a pain', does not even make sense, and the scepticism cannot be stated. But if these expressions do make sense then, *ipso facto*, there must be a way of telling, and the scepticism is self-refuting.

This looks very like the argument that a statement has no sense unless it is possible to prove it true or false. Malcolm seems to be saying that we have to be able to tell whether a man feels a pain before 'He feels a pain' can make sense, just as the verificationists argued that we have to be able to tell whether God exists before 'God exists' can make sense. However, I don't think Malcolm means to adopt a wholehearted verificationism; rather he thinks that his point follows from the first premiss of the private language argument. This explains why many who have discussed Wittgenstein's argument with special reference to Malcolm have come to the conclusion that it is another version of the verification theory of meaning. However, we saw (p. 77 above) that the first premiss of the private language argument was not that an expression is not genuinely meaningful unless we can establish whether what it says is true, but only that an expression is not genuinely meaningful unless we can establish whether it is being used correctly. Or, to put the point in terms of criteria, an expression is not genuinely meaningful unless there are criteria governing its use and application. This means that there must be criteria governing the use and application of such expressions as 'He feels a pain' or 'He is thinking about the Budget'. In order to understand what precisely this commits us to we must say something about what is meant by 'criteria'.

2. To begin with, we must distinguish criteria from (logical) conditions, from 'symptoms', as Wittgenstein calls them, and from evidence. For the sake of an example let us say that for a fire to be going is for there to be flames among the material of the fire, the wood, coal, or whatever it is, a flame being defined as a flickering tongue of light that emits heat. Thus a fire which emits heat and/or smoke but no flames is not 'going', in this sense, and a glow, however hot, is no more a flame than is a heatless flicker of fluorescent light.

A (logical) condition is some feature of a situation—a state of affairs, event, object, etc.—whose presence is either (logically) necessary or (logically) sufficient for that situation's being of a certain sort, for that situation's being such that a certain expression can correctly, truthfully, be applied to it. Thus it is a necessary condition of the fire's being going that there be heat coming from the fireplace; if no heat is coming then it follows necessarily that the fire is not going. It is a sufficient condition of the fire's being going that flames be visible in the fireplace; it follows necessarily from the fact that flames can be seen that the fire is going.

A symptom, on the other hand, is some feature of a situation which is always but contingently associated with that situation's being of a certain sort. Thus if there is a roaring noise in the back of the chimney whenever and only when the fire is going, this noise would be a symptom that the fire is going. This seems to me to be an odd use of 'symptom', but as I understand it it is what Wittgenstein means by the term. (*Blue and Brown Books*, Blackwell, p. 25. Quotations are from this page unless otherwise stated.) Actually Wittgenstein defines symptoms by reference to criteria, but I prefer to leave criteria out of it for the moment.

Finally, evidence is any feature which is positively correlated with a situation's being of a certain sort. If normally when the fire is going smoke comes out of the chimney, and vice versa, then this is evidence that the fire is going. Evidence does not constitute a symptom unless this correlation is universal, unless smoke comes out the chimney whenever and only when the fire is going. The chimney might be blocked when the fire is going, or the chimney might be on fire when the fire is not going, so smoke coming out of the chimney is evidence, not a symptom, that the fire is going.

There are two points to notice about these definitions. First, it might be said that a symptom need not be universally correlated with that of which it is a symptom; smoke coming out of the chimney could be a symptom that the fire is going so long as it 'coincided, in some way or other, with the phenomenon' of which it is a symptom. But despite Wittgenstein's words I think he does want to say that this coincidence must be universal, though not necessary. Otherwise I do not see how he can say what he goes on to say, that 'in practice, if you were asking which phenomenon is the defining criterion and which is a symptom, you would in most cases be unable to answer the question except by making an arbitrary decision *ad hoc*'. Clearly if a symptom can be used as a *defining* criterion[1] it must be universally correlated with that of which it is a symptom. Moreover, if the correlation is not universal it is hard to see why Wittgenstein should have preferred 'symptom' to the more usual term 'sign'.

---

[1] A defining criterion is one where the statement of it 'is a tautology . . . or a loose way of stating (a) definition'. I will come back to defining criteria in a moment.

Second, I have explicitly not defined conditions, symptoms, or evidence in terms of correlations which *we have discovered* to hold. No doubt if we are not aware of the correlation between A and B then we cannot use A as a symptom of or evidence for B, and in so far as Wittgenstein is concerned with what we actually use as symptoms, evidence, etc., so far his definition of symptoms in terms of what 'experience has taught us' is acceptable. But although whether or not we use A as symptom or evidence for B depends on whether we think there is a correlation between the two, whether or not A *is* symptom or evidence for B depends on whether this correlation holds, irrespective of whether we know it or not. The moment it turns out that the noise in the chimney is sometimes produced not by the fire but by the wind, that moment it turns out that the noise is not, and never was, a symptom that the fire is going. And the moment it turns out that there is little or no positive correlation between smoke coming out of the chimney and the fire's being going—perhaps the chimney is connected to more than one fireplace—that moment it turns out that the smoke is, and always was, weak or no evidence that the fire is going. If I have not discovered that these correlations do not hold, then I will go on using noise and smoke as symptom and evidence that the fire is going. But I will be mistaken—the noise is not a symptom, and the smoke is not evidence.

Now for criteria: basically criteria are features by which we tell that something is of a certain sort, but they differ from evidence and from symptoms in that the connexion between them and what they are criteria of is a logical, conceptual, connexion, one which depends not on the facts of the matter but on the meanings of the terms involved. So let us say that a criterion is some feature of a situation whose presence *means* that the situation is, to that extent, of a certain sort. Having four legs, for example, is a criterion of being a horse. It is neither a sufficient condition, for other things have four legs besides horses, nor a necessary condition, for freak five-legged horses are still horses. It is not even a symptom, at least not in the sense explained, and it is rather poor evidence, in that establishing that a thing has four legs is a long way from establishing that it is a horse, although it is a start. But although it is poor evidence, it is also more than evidence, inasmuch as having four legs is part of what we mean by 'horse', inasmuch as 'Horses are quadrupeds' is true by definition. In so far as a thing has four legs so far it is (what we call) a horse, so far it meets our definition of 'horse'. Of course it does not follow from the fact that it has four legs that it is a horse, for in so far as it has four legs it meets, to that extent, our definitions of many other things besides horses. Nor does it have to have four legs in order to be a horse; the doctrine of family resemblances reminds us that things do not have to satisfy all the criteria for *x*-ness in order to qualify as instances of *x*.

So criteria have two important features. First, like the things we use as symptoms and evidence, they provide ways of telling that something is of a certain sort. But second, unlike the things we use as symptoms and evidence, the link between criteria and that which they are criteria of is a logical link. So far as symptoms and evidence are concerned we will accept A as establishing B only in so far as we accept that there is a correlation between A and B. But where criteria are concerned there is no need to establish such a correlation, inasmuch as the connexion between A and B will be a matter of what we say—if it is A then, at any rate to that extent, it is what we call, what we mean by, a B.

Wittgenstein talks in particular about 'defining' criteria. It is not clear whether he thinks that all criteria are defining criteria, or whether he means the adjective to distinguish one important type of criteria. I prefer to take the latter course. Defining criteria are criteria from whose satisfaction it follows necessarily that the thing is of the kind in question. Wittgenstein says that if possessing the bacillus is a defining criterion of angina then ' "A man has angina if this bacillus is found in him" is a tautology or it is a loose way of stating the definition of angina'. Thus features which constitute defining criteria also constitute logically sufficient conditions. Given that 'hooved quadruped with flowing mane and tail' is an adequate definition of 'horse', then it can be taken as constituting a complex defining criterion of being a horse, and equally as constituting a complex logically sufficient condition of being a horse. But even if it follows logically from its being a hooved quadruped with a flowing mane and tail that it is a horse, it does not follow logically from its being a horse that it is a hooved quadruped with flowing mane and tail. A freak hairless horse is still a horse. Defining criteria do not constitute logically necessary conditions.

More importantly, defining criteria may constitute logically sufficient conditions, but not all logically sufficient conditions constitute defining criteria, or criteria at all. For not all logical conditions provide ways of telling. It may be a logically sufficient condition of some event's being a miracle that it be the result of divine intervention, but its being a result of divine intervention is not something we can use

in telling whether it is a miracle. Rather we will have to
establish on other grounds that it is a miracle before we can
accept that it is a result of divine intervention. This is the
important difference between criteria and logical conditions
—criteria enable us to *tell* whether a thing is of the kind
in question.

So far I have been speaking about the criteria for being
some thing, such as a horse, but most philosophers, following the later Wittgenstein, prefer to speak of the criteria for
the use of an expression, such as 'horse'. If by 'criteria for the
use of an expression' they mean that which tells us that it is
correct to call something by a particular name, or to apply
a particular description to it, then the criteria for being a
horse and the criteria for the use of the expression 'horse'
will be precisely the same. But in fact 'criteria for the use of
an expression' can be used to refer to criteria of a quite
different sort.

We have to distinguish between criteria which establish
that this is a horse, or what is called 'a horse', and criteria
which establish that the term 'horse' is being used correctly.
We have seen that there is a difference between using an
expression correctly, in the sense of in accordance with
the rules which govern its use and determine its meaning,
and using that expression to say something which is true.
Where we are concerned with such topics as understanding
and learning a language, we will be concerned not so much
with the criteria for whether what is said is true, as with the
criteria for whether what is said involves a correct use of the
expressions involved. These criteria must be different, since
it is possible to establish that a person is using an expression
such as 'God' or 'life on Venus' correctly, even where it is

not possible to establish whether what he says is true. I won't go into the difficult question of how precisely we do establish that a person is using a particular expression correctly. Presumably we have to discover what he means to assert, how he uses that expression on other occasions, and so on.

Now once we make this distinction we can see that if the private language argument is taken to show that there must be criteria governing the use of an expression, the criteria in question will be criteria for whether or not that expression is being used correctly, not criteria for whether or not what is said is true. That is, the first premiss of the private language argument can be stated as: there must be public criteria governing the use of any expression in a language. This does not mean that we must be able to tell whether any particular statement is true or false. That way lies verificationism. Nor does it mean that there must be discoverable circumstances which would make that statement a true statement. I doubt whether there are any criteria from whose satisfaction it follows that something is an act of black magic, or that someone is possessed by devils, but these expressions are meaningful none the less. If a statement is to be genuinely meaningful there must be circumstances in which it would be true and circumstances in which it would be false, but this does not mean that we must be able to tell which circumstances obtain.

So what the first premiss of the private language argument asserts is that there must be discoverable circumstances which would show that an expression is being used correctly, though not necessarily truthfully. Suppose, for example, that someone says of an old lady who lives alone and talks to her cat that she is a witch, meaning that she rides

dispute whether what he says is true or false

on a broom-stick and is in league with the devil. If we can establish that this is what he means, then we can establish that he is using the word 'witch' correctly, even though we may want to quarrel with his view of the old lady. The point is that if 'witch' is to be genuinely meaningful then we must be able to establish that this is what he is saying. But this is a long way from saying that we must be able to establish whether or not she is a witch. I am not sure what, if anything, would establish that she was in league with the devil. In other words, even if it is impossible to establish whether or not someone is a witch, it is not impossible to establish what counts as being a witch. If it were impossible to establish what counts as being a witch, what is meant by calling someone a witch, then it would be impossible to explain, teach, or check the use, the meaning, of that word, 'witch'. Thus the meaning of 'witch' must be publicly ex-plicable; there must be public phenomena by reference to which we can teach and learn the meaning of the word. We will see that this is the important point, the point which each of the three arguments under discussion tries to make too much of.

3. The argument from criteria is that there are and must be criteria for the ascription of conscious states and processes to others. We must have criteria if we are to understand what such ascriptions mean, and these criteria will provide us with absolutely conclusive ways of telling that other beings possess conscious states and processes. 'The satisfac-tion of the criteria of y establishes the existence of y beyond question. . . . It will not make sense for one to suppose that another person is not in pain if one's criterion of his being

in pain is satisfied' (*Knowledge and Certainty*, p. 113). Nevertheless the satisfaction of the criteria does not entail that a
pain is felt: 'A criterion is satisfied *only in certain circumstances*.'
There are circumstances, for example, during the perfor-
mance of a play, where the criteria are not satisfied as they
ordinarily are, or as we might prefer to put it, where the
satisfaction of the normal criteria is not sufficient to establish
that the person does feel a pain. Moreover, we cannot specify
in advance precisely what these circumstances are. This
makes us inclined to say, 'If it does not *follow* from his
behaviour and circumstances that he is in pain, then how
can it ever be *certain* that he is in pain? . . . It *looks* as if the
conclusion ought to be that we cannot 'completely verify'
that he is in pain' (p. 115). In his review of the *Philosophical
Investigations* Malcolm confesses that he is not sure how to
answer this, and he falls back on the claim that doubting has
an end: 'There is a concept of certainty in these language-
games only because we stop short of what is conceivable'
(p. 116).

   Yet to say this is to concede the sceptic's point. It is to
admit that although we claim certainty in our knowledge
of other minds, it is nevertheless conceivable that we are
mistaken in taking another person's behaviour and circumstances as conclusive evidence that he feels a pain. I
doubt whether Malcolm really means to concede this point.
For he does say, 'It will *not make sense* for one to suppose that
another person is not in pain if one's criterion of his being
in pain is satisfied' (my italics), and his article on 'Our
Knowledge of Other Minds' is based on the principle that
ascriptions of conscious states and processes to others are
meaningless unless based on criteria: 'If Mill has no criterion

for the existence of feelings other than his own then in that sense he does not understand the sentence "That human figure has feelings"' (p. 131).

It is never explicitly stated, but I think the point must be that even if it is in some sense conceivable that a man might exhibit all the usual marks of feeling a pain and yet not be feeling one, this state of affairs is unstatable, cannot be described. Even though it is possible in principle that the criteria should be satisfied and the man not feel a pain, it is not possible for us to talk about his feeling or not feeling a pain unless we accept the criteria as establishing that he does feel a pain. Since we cannot talk about his pain unless we accept the criteria, it does not make sense to say of someone who satisfies the criteria that he might not feel a pain. This conclusion is much the same as that of the private language argument. The sceptic's premiss, that there might be all the usual marks of pain but no pain, is not self-contradictory, but it cannot be stated. As an earlier Wittgenstein might have put it, and as the later Wittgenstein seems inclined to put it, the sceptic tries to say what cannot be said.

All of this depends on the claim that our ascriptions of conscious states and processes to others cannot make sense unless we have criteria for ascribing them to others. If by 'criteria' Malcolm means criteria which establish that someone feels a pain, then this claim is tantamount to verificationism: a statement does not make sense unless we have some way of telling whether it is true. So if Malcolm does not mean to adopt verificationism, by 'criteria' he must mean criteria which establish that the expression is being used correctly. Let us agree with Malcolm, and with the private language argument, that if we are to speak about being a male and unmarried is to be a bachelor.

feeling pains at all, there must be criteria for use of the expression 'feels a pain', criteria which establish that the expression is being used correctly. Whether or not the criteria must establish this 'beyond question' I do not know. I think there are criteria which establish beyond question that a certain expression is being used correctly, but I don't know of any argument to show what Malcolm seems to want to say, that there *must be* such criteria. The premiss of the private language argument is only that there must be criteria, not that these criteria must establish beyond question.

However, the important point is that even if we agree that there must be criteria which establish that the expression is being used correctly if we are to speak about feeling pains at all, it does not follow that there must be criteria which establish that a person does feel a pain. We could establish that people are using the expression 'feels a pain' correctly even if no one ever felt pains, just as we can establish that people are using the word 'unicorn' correctly even though no unicorns exist. To move, as Malcolm does, from the claim that we must be able to establish that this is the correct way to use 'He feels a pain' to the claim that we must be able to establish whether he does feel a pain, is to move from an important—indeed the important—truth about our use of such expressions, to a quite unacceptable verificationism.

It might be said that we have here a distinction with a difference, in that if there are ways of telling that the application of 'feels a pain' to a certain person is correct, then there will be ways of telling whether that person does feel a pain, viz. when the conditions for the correct application of the expression are satisfied. If we can establish that it is correct to say of Jones that he feels a pain, then we can establish that he does feel a pain. But this is to ignore the distinction between using an expression correctly and saying something which is true. The word 'pain' is being used correctly when it is used to refer to a certain sort of private sensation, the sensation produced by wounds and injuries and resulting in groans and cries. There are public criteria by which we can tell whether the word is being used in this way. If, for example, someone thought that 'pain' referred to bleeding wounds, or to writhing limbs, or to the uttering of groans, then his very use of the word 'pain' would show that he was not using the term correctly. He would say things like 'Listen to his pain' or 'I can't see any pain', and we would have to explain to him that 'pain' referred not to visible or audible phenomena but to something else, something which is felt, and felt by only the one person.

So just as there are public criteria which establish that a sensation is a pain sensation, so there are public criteria, in particular the way one uses the word, which establish that the word 'pain' is being used correctly, to refer to a private sensation. However, this does not mean that there are public criteria which establish, 'beyond question', that a sensation is felt. The crux of the matter is whether we can tell that a man is referring to a sensation, without being able to tell whether the sensation referred to exists. If we can do this then the fact that there are and must be criteria which establish that the word 'pain' is being used correctly does not show that there are and must be criteria which establish that another feels a pain. And clearly we can do it. Suppose a dentist gives a local anaesthetic to a particularly nervous patient. Despite the anaesthetic the patient claims to feel a pain every time the dentist starts to drill. The dentist can speak of this alleged pain and so, in consequence of the logical grammar of the word 'pain', refer to a sensation about whose existence he is uncertain, in just the way that, in speaking of God, a man may refer to a being about whose existence he is uncertain. Of course if there is no pain, if there is no God, then the reference is 'unsuccessful', but I trust that no one is going to say that an unsuccessful reference necessarily involves a breach of meaning.

4. Malcolm's basic mistake is the failure to notice the distinction between using an expression correctly and using it to say something true.[1] This is true even of his monograph on *Dreaming* (Routledge & Kegan Paul), despite the fact that he there explicitly mentions the distinction. Perhaps it is worth looking at his argument in some detail. His thesis is 'that if anyone holds that dreams are identical with, or composed of thoughts, impressions, feelings, images and so on (here one may supply whatever other mental nouns one likes, except "dreams") occurring in sleep, then his view is false' (p. 52). This paradoxical view leads to even more paradoxical conclusions—for example, that any attempt to explain what a dream is would be unintelligible, or that while dreams occur in or during sleep they do not occur in physical time—and it has been said that all this, in itself, provides an effective *reductio ad absurdum* of Malcolm's form of argument.

In brief the argument is that while it is true by definition

[1] J. W. Cornman, 'Malcolm's Mistaken Memory', *Analysis*, 1965, argues that the same mistake underlies Malcolm's discussion of scepticism concerning memory.

that dreams occur in sleep, this shows that dreams cannot consist of or involve judgements, thoughts, images, feelings, or anything of that sort, since the idea that they might occur in sleep is unintelligible. This is first argued with reference to judgements:

It is nonsensical to suppose that while a person is asleep he could make *any* judgement. Remember that the logical absurdity detected in the sentence 'I am asleep' amounts to this: that in order for the sentence to have a *correct* use one would sometimes have to say it when the thing one said was *true*. We noticed that it would be self-contradictory to *verify* that a man was both asleep and judging that he was, because whatever in his behaviour showed he was making the judgement would equally show he was not asleep. Now this would be so *whatever* the judgement was. In order to know that he had made any judgement one would have to know that he had said certain words and that he had been aware of saying them. But whatever it was in his demeanour that revealed his awareness of saying them would also establish that he was not asleep. To verify that he was both asleep and making a judgement one would have to verify that he was both aware and not aware of saying certain words. It would not matter whether the words were 'It is raining' or 'My wife is jealous' or any other words. It would be self-contradictory to verify that he made *any* judgement while asleep.[1]

At first sight the argument may seem to be that the notion of making a judgement while asleep is self-contradictory, since in order to make a judgement one must be aware of what one is judging, whereas being asleep is incompatible with being aware of anything. The answer to this would have to be that although being aware, in the sense in which one must be aware of something if one is to judge, may be

[1] p. 36, Malcolm's italics.

incompatible with being *sound* asleep, awareness is not in-compatible with sleep as such. There is an obvious sense in which the sleep-walker, or the man who has a dream built around the noise of the alarm-clock, is to some extent aware of his surroundings. However, this is not Malcolm's argu-ment. He explicitly says that the notion of judging while asleep is not itself self-contradictory. Rather the argument is that the notion of judging—or having images, thoughts, feelings, etc.—while asleep is nonsensical because nothing could establish that a man was both asleep and judging. Nothing could establish this because anything that showed that he was judging would at the same time show that he was not asleep.

Suppose I claim to have dreamt that I saw the Prime Minister being chased by a pterodactyl. Indeed I claim that while asleep I had various images and thought to myself, or judged, that the Prime Minister was being chased by a pterodactyl. This claim would be unverifiable. If you doubted whether I had dreamt or judged it, the only way to establish whether I had or had not would be to question me further or to extract the truth by torture, and any claim that I had not dreamt it could be as suspect as my original claim that I had. Moreover, if I begin to wonder whether I did have that dream, whether I am perhaps remembering a newspaper cartoon rather than a dream which occurred while I was asleep, then there is no way in which I can settle my doubt. Even if there was a newspaper cartoon I might also have dreamt about it. There is a definite sense in which it is impossible to establish whether a man did judge, or think, or have images, or even dream, while he was asleep, as he thinks he did.

Nevertheless I would not go so far as to say that the idea of establishing that he did judge, etc., while asleep is self-contradictory. Even if we concentrate on behavioural evidence, as Malcolm does, it is not true that any animate behaviour whatsoever counts against the claim that someone is asleep. If a person curls himself into a ball, shivers, and mutters about rugs and hot-water bottles, though in all other respects he seems asleep, this would ordinarily be taken as evidence in support of his later claim that while asleep he thought or judged that he was freezing to death. Where some behaviour counts in favour of the claim that he made a judgement, and other behaviour counts in favour of the claim that he was asleep, no self-contradiction is involved. True, his moving and shivering and muttering would count against the claim that he was sound asleep, but not all sleeping is sound sleeping, and we need have no qualms about making it true by definition that one does not judge or think or dream while one is sound asleep. I am inclined to think that the main reason for insisting that it is self-contradictory to verify that a person is both asleep and judging is a concealed acceptance of the view that the notion of judging while asleep is itself self-contradictory.

However, whether we agree about the self-contradiction or not, let us agree that it is impossible to verify whether a man has judged while he was asleep. The important question is whether this shows that the suggestion that he has is nonsensical. Once again we seem to be coming very close to verificationism, and in fact Malcolm's argument seems to be that for the suggestion to make sense, 'He has made a judgement while asleep' would have to have a correct use, and that to have a correct use we must be able to tell when it is being used truly. What Malcolm actually says is 'in order for the sentence to have a *correct* use one would sometimes have to say it when the thing one said was true' (p. 36), but this may be meant only to be a special feature of 'I am asleep'. Otherwise 'The Prime Minister is being chased by a pterodactyl' would have to be nonsensical, a sentence without a correct use since on no occasion is it said when true! Presumably Malcolm means to say that for a sentence to have a correct use one must know when it would be true. Now this is ambiguous between knowing, in a particular case, whether it is true or not, and knowing what, if it occurred, would make it true. If 'For a sentence to have a correct use one must know when it would be true' means that a statement is not genuinely meaningful unless we can establish *whether* it is true or false, then this claim is clearly false. But if it means that a statement is not genuinely meaningful unless we can establish *under what conditions* it would be true or false, then the claim is correct. If we are to understand a statement we must know and be able to tell what it asserts, but we need not know or be able to tell whether it is true or false.[1] So far as judging while asleep goes, even if it is impossible to tell with any certainty whether it has happened or whether the person merely thinks or says that it has, we do know what would count as its happening, and hence we do know what would make the appropriate sentence true. That is all that is necessary for the sentence to have a correct use.

[1] Strawson ('Truth: A Reconsideration of Austin's Views', *Philosophical Quarterly*, 1965) has shown how this same ambiguity underlies Austin's version of the correspondence theory of truth. Austin thought of his 'descriptive conventions' as determining whether a statement is true or false, but in fact they determine only what the statement asserts, i.e. in what n ditions it would be true or false.

Thus we slide into verificationism, as Malcolm does here, only if we fail[*] to notice the distinction between using a sentence correctly and using it to say something true, if we think that to know whether a sentence is being used correctly we must be able to tell, at least in some cases, when, i.e. whether, it is true. The most that is necessary is that we know when, i.e. under what conditions, it is true. Nevertheless, as mentioned before, Malcolm is aware that there is this distinction between a correct use and a true use, although he thinks that using a sentence correctly presupposes using it truthfully, and hence that knowing how to use it correctly presupposes being able to tell whether what it says is true. He says:

Using a sentence *correctly* and using it to make a *true* statement are different concepts, but the former depends on the latter in the same sense that the concept of an order depends on the concept of obeying an order: it could not be that the people of a tribe gave orders to one another which no one ever or hardly ever obeyed, for there could be no justification for describing the sounds they made as *orders* (§345). I am accepting Wittgenstein's thesis that 'if a language is to be a means of communication there must be agreement not only in definitions but also . . . in judgements' (§242). (pp. 9–10. The references are to the *Philosophical Investigations*, Part I.)

It is not clear precisely what this shows. Certainly if our words are to have a clear sense we must agree, to a considerable extent, not only in what we say we mean, but also in what we actually say. If we seldom if ever agreed about what to say of this or that state of affairs, then we could scarcely communicate at all. This does not mean that we must agree over the truth of every particular statement. More importantly, it does not mean that our statements have to be true, even where we all agree that they are true. It means only that we must, on the whole, agree about what is true, whether it actually is true or not. The fact that we all agree that a statement is true does not mean that it is true.

Now it might be said that if we all accept a statement as true in certain circumstances—as we all accept it as true that a man feels a pain when he is bleeding and groaning—then it makes no sense to suggest that that statement might be false in those circumstances. Our ways of speaking are to be accepted as they stand; all we can say is that this is what we do say, that 'the language-game is played'. But it is surely not enough to say merely that the language-game is played where what is at stake is not meaning but truth, not what our statements assert but whether they are correct. Thus the fact that we all claim to know something shows us what counts as knowledge, what conditions have to be satisfied before we will accept that something is known. But it does not show that we do know it, because it does not show that what we claim to know is in fact true. There was a time when everyone claimed to know that the earth was flat. Thus the appeal to what we say shows only what our claim to know means; it does not show whether that claim is correct. Similarly the fact that in certain circumstances we all agree that *p* is true does nothing to show that *p* is true, unless what we *mean* by *p* is simply that these circumstances do hold. I think Malcolm would agree that a person's behaviour and circumstances are not what we *mean* by 'He feels a pain', so the fact that in these circumstances we all agree that he feels a pain does not, by itself, show that he does feel one.

I have argued that the argument from criteria, and Malcolm's apparent verificationism, spring from a misreading of the fact that there must be criteria for the use of all expressions, including 'He feels a pain'. We will see that this fact has important consequences for the other minds problem, consequences that Malcolm himself may well be aware of, even though it does not support the conclusion that we cannot speak about pains, or conscious states, at all unless we have some means of establishing beyond question that a certain person feels a pain or possesses some particular conscious state.

CHAPTER VII

The Argument from Persons

1. THE argument from persons might equally well be called the argument from 'Persons'. It is the argument suggested by Strawson in his article of that title, and in the largely similar chapter in his book *Individuals*.[1] The main point that Strawson wishes to make is that the concept of a person, being the concept of something which possesses both conscious states and corporeal characteristics, is as he puts it 'logically primitive'. By this he means that the concept of a person should not be thought of as a construction out of the two concepts of a body and a consciousness, because the concept of a consciousness, as such, is attainable only via the concept of a person. That is, we need the concept of a person if we are to form the concept of a consciousness, and so we cannot use the latter in any reductive analysis of the former. Similarly, our concepts of the various conscious states and processes, such as feeling a pain or feeling depressed, are dependent upon our concept of a person, in that we could not have these concepts unless we ascribed them to things possessing corporeal characteristics as well as these conscious states and processes. Indeed, not merely must we ascribe conscious states to beings who also possess corporeal characteristics, it seems that we must ascribe them on the basis of

[1] *Individuals* (Methuen), Chap. 3. All references in this chapter will be to this book, unless otherwise stated. The article 'Persons' was originally printed in *Minnesota Publications in the Philosophy of Science*, vol. 2.

corporeal characteristics. Corporeal characteristics, particularly behaviour, must provide a 'logically adequate criterion' for the ascription of conscious states to others. This is the point that most concerns us.

Strawson's argument is extremely difficult to isolate, but as I understand it it runs as follows:

(1) If I am to speak about conscious states at all, even my own, I must be prepared to ascribe them to others.
(2) If I am to ascribe them to others I must be able to identify them in others.
(3) This identification is (must be?) done by reference to physical characteristics, particularly behaviour.
(4) Therefore behaviour must provide a logically adequate criterion for the ascription of conscious states to others.

One of the main difficulties is that Strawson nowhere explains what precisely he means by a 'logically adequate criterion'. I am sure that he does not want to say that behaviour, even together with other corporeal characteristics, provides a logically adequate (= sufficient?) *condition* for the possession of conscious states by others. That is, he does not want to say that it follows, as a matter of logic, from the fact that a being is behaving in a certain way that, for example, he feels a pain. He is not saying that the sceptical suggestion that a man might exhibit the behaviour and yet not feel a pain is self-contradictory. Rather he seems to be saying that the suggestion that the man's behaviour does not, 'in the last resort', prove that he does feel a pain is incoherent, perhaps even self-contradictory. Behaviour is a logically adequate *criterion* for the ascription of conscious states to others. What follows, as a matter of logic, from his behaviour is not that he does feel a pain, but that we are in a position to tell, to know, that he feels a pain. What is incoherent, because self-contradictory, is not so much 'He exhibits pain-behaviour but feels no pain' as 'He exhibits pain-behaviour but we do not know whether he feels a pain'. And if this can be established it will be enough to refute the scepticism we discussed in Chapter IV.

Let us look at the argument step by step.

2. Strawson describes the first step of his argument as 'a very simple, but in this question a very central, thought: viz. that it is a necessary condition of one's ascribing states of consciousness, experiences, to oneself, in the way that one does, that one should also ascribe them, or be prepared to ascribe them, to others who are not oneself' (p. 99). At first sight this seems to be some form of the Polar Contrasts argument: that there is no sense in talking about 'me' and 'mine' unless there are 'you' and 'yours' and/or 'them' and 'theirs' to contrast 'me' and 'mine' with. Thus p. 109: 'If *only* mine, then *not* mine at all.' Nevertheless a Polar Contrasts argument will not establish Strawson's point. For although a contrast between me and mine and what is not me and mine may be necessary if 'me' and 'mine' are to have any real sense, it is not necessary that the contrast be with other people, other possessors of conscious states. Clearly there is little point in talking of myself and my conscious states as opposed to other beings and their conscious states if there are no other conscious beings, but this does not mean that I cannot speak of myself and my conscious states as opposed to other non-conscious bodies.

However, I doubt whether it is this Polar Contrasts argument that Strawson means to put forward. Rather the point is, as Strawson puts it in the footnote to p. 99, 'a purely logical one: the idea of a predicate is correlative with that of a *range* of distinguishable individuals of which the predicate can be significantly, though not necessarily truly, affirmed'. This logical point, I take it, is that if any predicate or quality x is ascribed to an object it will be in virtue of certain conditions a, b, c, etc., which that object is believed to satisfy. So any object which can possess a, b, c, etc., can, rightly or wrongly but in any event significantly, be called x, and any object which does possess a, b, c, etc., can correctly be called x. No predicate has a logically unique application.

This point seems quite acceptable. To put it very simply: if we are even to state the other minds problem we must at least have the concept of conscious states belonging to others, of conscious states which I do not have. Even if we deny that this concept is instantiated, we still have to allow that there are conditions under which it would be correct to ascribe conscious states to others (cf. Aune, 'The Problem of Other Minds', *Philosophical Review*, 1961, pp. 377–8). So if I am to say of anything, even myself, that it feels a pain, there must be some condition whose satisfaction in this case makes it correct, true, to say that it feels a pain, and whose satisfaction in any other case would mean that it would be correct to say of that other thing that it felt a pain. In saying that I feel a pain I assert that the condition is satisfied, and if the condition were to be satisfied for anything else then that something else could also, and truly, be said to feel a pain. There are two things to notice about this.

First, as Strawson allows, although he does not think the point important, this does not mean that I actually do ascribe conscious states to others. It means only that I must be prepared to, in the sense that I allow that there are circumstances under which it would be correct to do so, even if I think that these circumstances never occur. Second, it has not been shown that I must know whether these circumstances do occur (cf. Ayer, *Concept of a Person*, Macmillan, pp. 104–6). Even if there must be conditions under which it would be correct to ascribe conscious states to others, it may still be that we cannot tell when these conditions are satisfied—as seems to be the case, for example, with the conditions for something's being an act of divine intervention.

Of course we might argue that if I am to ascribe conscious states to myself, then just as I must be prepared to ascribe them to others when the same conditions are satisfied, so I must be prepared to ascribe them to others when the same criteria are satisfied. But Strawson for one, and Malcolm for another, cannot argue in this way. For Strawson puts great emphasis on the fact that what he calls P-predicates[1] have two sets of logically adequate criteria, one set for self-ascription and one for ascription to others. This in itself does not debar him from arguing that when I ascribe pain to myself I commit myself to ascribing pain to anything else which satisfies my criterion for the ascription of pain. For

---

[1] P-predicates are predicates we ascribe only to things to which we also ascribe states of consciousness. They include not only such things as 'feels a pain' or 'sees a horse', but also 'is smiling' or 'is going for a walk'. They are contrasted with M-predicates, predicates which can be applied both to things which possess states of consciousness and to things which do not, e.g. 'weighs 10 stone' or 'is in the drawing room'. See *Individuals*, p. 104.

even if there are two sets of criteria it will remain true that 'pain' is correctly ascribed in however so many cases either set of criteria is satisfied. Nevertheless Strawson is trying to prove that behaviour is a logically adequate criterion for the ascription of pain, and he is also saying that behaviour is not the criterion for the self-ascription of pain. But if behaviour is not the criterion for the self-ascription of pain, the argument that self-ascription presupposes other-ascription cannot possibly prove that behaviour is a logically adequate criterion for the other-ascription of pain. For Malcolm, on the other hand, I do not ascribe pain to myself on the basis of criteria at all.

Nevertheless the main point has been established: that if I am to speak about conscious states at all, if I am even to ascribe them to myself, I must at least be prepared to ascribe them to others.

3. The next step in the argument is the claim that if I am to ascribe conscious states to others I must be able to identify them in others. What Strawson actually says is, 'Clearly there is no sense in talking of identifiable individuals of a special type, a type, namely, such that they possess both M-predicates and P-predicates, unless there is in principle some way of telling, with regard to any individual of that type, and any P-predicate, whether that individual possesses that P-predicate' (p. 105). Once again this looks very like verificationism; it looks very much as if Strawson is saying, 'We cannot significantly say that another does or does not feel a pain unless we can tell whether he does', just as the verificationists said, 'We cannot significantly say that God does or does not exist unless we can tell whether he does.'

However, I don't think this is what Strawson really wants to say. He is concerned with identification, not verification, and his point is, I assume, that we must be able to identify the particular conscious state which we ascribe to another. The difficulty is to see how this point is supposed to be established. It may simply be a consequence of the point made in the first chapter, and itself unargued, that we cannot speak about something unless we can identify things of the kind in question: 'What could we mean by claiming to acknowledge the existence of a class of particular things and to talk to each other about members of this class, if we qualified the claim by adding that it was in principle impossible for any one of us to make any other of us understand which member, or members, of this class he was at any time talking about?' (p. 16). Thus we cannot speak of Tom's pain, and hence can neither ascribe pain to him nor deny that ascription, unless we can identify Tom's pain, which we do by identifying Tom.

But whether the point is argued for or not, it seems to be acceptable enough. If we are to talk about conscious states belonging to other beings we must be able to identify the beings to whom we are ascribing them, and we must be able to identify what it is that we are ascribing to them. Nevertheless once we distinguish identification from verification we will realize that all this means is that we must be able to tell what, and which one, we are talking about; it does not mean that we must be able to tell whether what we say is true.

4. The third step in the main argument is the claim that this identification of conscious states in others must be done by reference to physical characteristics, such as a person's

behaviour. Perhaps all the argument needs is the point that, as a matter of fact, we do identify conscious states by reference to behaviour, but I think Strawson means to argue for the stronger point. He says (p. 105 and p. 106) that this is a consequence of his wider argument for the primitiveness of the concept of a person. As I understand it this wider argument runs as follows:

(1) Conscious states can be identified only as belonging to some particular subject of experience, some possessor of conscious states.

(2) A possessor of conscious states can be identified only if it also possesses physical characteristics.

(3) Therefore conscious states cannot be identified unless they belong to something which also possesses physical characteristics—a person.

And the further conclusion to be drawn from this is:

(4) Conscious states cannot be identified except via physical characteristics such as behaviour.

This argument is completely unacceptable. The first premiss, to begin with, is simply false, given the relevant sense of 'identify'. I might, for example, identify a conscious state as the one causally dependent upon a certain brain state; this would not be to identify the conscious state by reference to what possesses it, unless one held that conscious states are possessed by brain states (!). Or I might draw something, look at it, destroy the drawing, and then identify the conscious state as the only state of perceiving that drawing that ever occurred. Strawson's argument against the possibility of identifying conscious states except by reference to what possesses them depends on an ambiguity in the term 'identify'.

This comes out clearly if we consider his argument against the 'No-ownership Theorist', an argument which is designed to show that states of consciousness 'owe their identity' to what possesses them, and consequently that their ownership is logically non-transferable, i.e., in my terms, that they are l-private. Strawson says, 'If we think . . . of the requirements of identifying reference in speech to *particular* states of consciousness, or private experiences, we see that such particulars cannot be thus identifyingly referred to except as the states or experiences *of* some identified *person*. States, or experiences, one might say, *owe* their identity as particulars to the identity of the person whose states or experiences they are' (p. 97). But we must distinguish between a thing's being identified, in the sense of being identifyingly referred to, and a thing's being identified, in the sense of its owing its identity to something. I may identify Joe Bloggs as the man in the green tie—and thus make an identifying reference to him— but Joe Bloggs does not owe his identity to the fact that he wears a green tie. Similarly the fact that experiences 'owe their identity as particulars to the identity of the person whose experiences they are' does not mean that they cannot be 'identifyingly referred to except as the experiences of some identified person'. Strawson may succeed in establishing that experiences must owe their identity to what possesses them, but he does not establish that experiences can be identified only by reference to what possesses them—although, naturally, this will be one way in which they can be identifyingly referred to, i.e. as the experiences of this or that person.

The second step in the argument is that a possessor of conscious states can be identified only if it also possesses physical characteristics. The point is, I take it, that we cannot identify a thing unless it can, directly or indirectly, be 'tied down' to something which has a determinate spatio-temporal location. But why should we not ascribe conscious states not directly to something possessing physical characteristics, but to a consciousness, a pure ego, which is itself identified by reference to something possessing physical characteristics? That is, we might ascribe particular conscious states and processes to the consciousness or ego belonging to a certain human body, and we could then identify that consciousness by reference to that body. Strawson thinks we cannot do this, because he thinks that in identifying such a consciousness I would have to refer to *my*self, to *my* experiences, when the possibility of identifying a possessor of conscious states is precisely what is at issue. If I don't refer to myself, or my experiences, then

the most I may be allowed to have noted is that experiences, *all* experiences, stand in a special relation to body M, that body M is unique in just this way. . . . The proffered explanation runs: 'Another subject of experience is distinguished and identified as the subject of those experiences which stand in the same unique causal relationship to body N as *my* experiences stand in to body M.' And the objection is 'But what is the word "my" doing in this explanation?' It is not as though the explanation could get on without this word' (p. 101).

But this goes much too far. The most that I can have noted is not that *all* experiences stand in a certain relation to body M, but only that all the experiences I[1] know of stand in that

---

[1] The presence of the word 'I' here need not worry us, but if it does we can replace it by individual references to this, that, and the other conscious state—the various conscious states that happen to stand in that relation to body M.

relation to body M. There may well be other experiences, of which as yet I know nothing, which are not related to body M at all. Nor is it true to say that the explanation cannot get along without the word 'my'. We need say only 'Another subject of experience is distinguished and identified as the subject of those experiences which stand in the same unique causal relationship to body N as the experiences causally dependent upon body M stand in to body M'. Or more simply: 'A particular subject of experience is distinguished and identified as the subject of those experiences causally dependent upon a particular body.' I suspect that Strawson thinks we cannot say this because it would make the connexion between the experiences and the body M an analytic one, but this is a mistake. What is analytic is not the connexion between the experiences and body M, but the connexion between being causally dependent upon body M and standing in that unique relationship to body M. Compare: 'Your mother is the person who stands in the same relationship to you as the person who bore me stands in to me.' This does not mean that the relationship between my mother and myself is an analytic one; what is analytic is the relationship between being the person who bore me and being my mother.

The basic mistake is, once again, the failure to distinguish 'conscious states owe their identity to what they belong to' from 'conscious states cannot be identifyingly referred to, except as belonging to such and such'. For, assuming that I cannot identify a conscious state except by reference to what possesses it, it follows that I cannot ascribe a conscious state to anything unless I can already identify its possessor, and therefore that I cannot identify the possessor by reference to the conscious states. But the assumption is false. What is true is that conscious states owe their identity to what they belong to, which means that if we ascribe conscious states to pure consciousnesses themselves identified by reference to physical bodies, then it becomes impossible for this particular conscious state to be causally dependent on any other body, just as it is impossible for this particular frown to be found on any other face. But there is nothing particularly worrying about this.

My doubts about Strawson's argument extend to the third step, the conclusion that conscious states must belong to, be ascribed to, persons. Even given the first two steps I am not sure that this follows. Even if we do have to ascribe conscious states to things which also possess physical characteristics we might ascribe them not to persons, but to physical, human, bodies. It might be said that this is equivalent to ascribing them to persons, since a body to which a conscious state is ascribed will be a conscious body, and a person is nothing but a conscious body. I am not sure about this, but I doubt whether Strawson, for one, would accept this identification of a person with a conscious body. A conscious body is, but does not possess, a body; a person possesses, but is not, a body. When I refer to 'I' I do not refer to 'this body' (nor, for that matter, to 'this consciousness'); I refer to 'this person'. And so on.

However, allowing that there is a difference between 'conscious body' and 'person', Strawson's argument nowhere rules out the possibility of ascribing conscious states to bodies rather than to persons. The argument against the 'No-ownership Theorist' may seem to show that we cannot ascribe conscious states to bodies, but in fact what it shows is that we cannot do this and still maintain, as the No-ownership Theorist does, that the connexion between the two is purely contingent. The point is that if we ascribe conscious states to bodies it will then be a necessary fact that this particular state belongs to this particular body. But this does not mean that we cannot ascribe conscious states to bodies. In fact many will regard it as a good reason for doing so.

So Strawson's argument is a complete muddle, due to the failure to distinguish the two senses of 'identify'. And even if he does succeed in showing that conscious states must 'owe their identity' to their possessors, things which also possess physical properties, this would be quite irrelevant to the present problem. It can hardly be maintained that we cannot speak about some thing unless we can tell what it owes its identity to. Clearly I can talk about Joe Bloggs without having to discover what makes him this person and not his brother Bert Bloggs, just as I can talk about this or that firm without being quite sure what makes it this firm rather than another firm (is a firm under completely new management the same firm or not?).

We have, then, to return to the modified point: that as a matter of fact it is by reference to behaviour that we identify conscious states in others. That is, it is by reference to his behaviour, what he says and does, that I tell that what is happening is that he feels a pain, and that Tom is the one who is feeling it.

5. The question now is whether any of this establishes Strawson's conclusion, that behaviour must provide a 'logically adequate criterion' for the ascription of conscious states

to others. Let us agree that I must be at least prepared to ascribe conscious states to others if I am to speak about conscious states at all, even my own; and that if we are to ascribe conscious states to others we must be able to tell who we are ascribing them to, and what we are ascribing to them; and that it is by reference to a person and his behaviour that we tell who we are ascribing them to, and what we are ascribing to them. The most that seems to follow is that it is only because we accept behaviour as a means of referring to conscious states in others that we are able to talk about conscious states, even our own, at all. This is a long way from showing that behaviour must provide a logically adequate way of telling that others do possess these conscious states.

If we are to talk about the conscious states of others we must be able to identify who and what we are talking about. But this has nothing to do with whether what we say is true. I take it that Strawson does not mean that we cannot talk about something unless we can tell whether or not it exists; I take it that he means merely that we cannot talk about something unless we can tell what it is that we are talking about, regardless of whether it exists, and regardless of whether what we say is true. Strawson hopes to show that we cannot ascribe conscious states to anything, even ourselves, unless we have some 'logically adequate' way of telling that our ascriptions of conscious states to others are correct, that those others do possess those conscious states. But all that he says is that we have a way of identifying, referring to, those conscious states which, rightly or wrongly, we ascribe to other people. Strawson does not notice the gap between the two because he does not seem to distinguish between 'tell' in the sense of 'identify' and 'tell' in the sense of 'verify', between saying that we must be able to tell what we are talking about and saying that we must be able to tell whether what we say is true.

I think Strawson fails to notice this crucial, and rather obvious, distinction between verification and identification because he is inclined to make too much of his original point that if we are to speak about conscious states at all we must be prepared to ascribe them to others. This comes out clearly on pp. 105–6, where Strawson argues explicitly that behaviour must be more than a sign of the presence of conscious states in others. His reason is that since we must be able to ascribe conscious states to others before we can talk about conscious states at all, we must have some means of ascribing them to others before we could establish that behaviour was a sign. But as we saw in Section 2 above, what Strawson shows is that we must be prepared to ascribe conscious states to others, only in the sense that we must allow that there are conditions under which it would be correct to do so. This does not mean that we must be able to tell when those conditions are satisfied, and to say that there must be *conditions* under which it would be correct to ascribe various conscious states to others is not to say that we must have *criteria* which establish that it would be correct, true, to do so. Indeed we saw (pp. 136–7 above) that Strawson's argument could not possibly show that we must have criteria which establish that others possess various conscious states.

Everything turns on Strawson's claim that 'There is no sense in the idea of ascribing states of consciousness to one-self, or at all, unless the ascriber knows how to ascribe at least some states of consciousness to others' (p. 106). If this is to show that behaviour provides a logically adequate criterion for the ascription of conscious states to others, it must mean that we cannot ascribe conscious states at all unless we have logically adequate ways of telling that various people possess various conscious states. But all that the 'purely logical' point on p. 99 establishes is that it must be possible, make sense, to ascribe conscious states to others. And all that the point about identification amounts to is that we must be able to identify which conscious state and which person we are talking about. To move from these to the stronger claim that if we are to talk about conscious states at all we must be able to tell whether others do possess various conscious states, is to opt for a grossly implausible verificationism. Strawson does not see this, partly because he does not clearly distinguish verification and identification, partly because he places too much weight on the claim that we must be prepared to ascribe conscious states to other possessors, and no doubt partly because of the vagueness of the expression 'knows how to ascribe'. What is necessary if we are to ascribe conscious states to others, or ourselves, is that we know what we are saying. It is not necessary that we know whether what we say is true.

Strawson's arguments may be unacceptable, but his conclusion may still be correct—behaviour may provide a logically adequate criterion for the ascription of conscious states to others. It all depends on what we mean by 'logically adequate criterion'.

CHAPTER VIII

The Justification of our Belief in Other Minds

1. WHAT precisely is a 'logically adequate criterion'? On p. 110 of *Individuals* Strawson says:

> If one is playing a game of cards, the distinctive markings of a certain card constitute a logically adequate criterion for calling it, say, the Queen of Hearts; but in calling it this, in the context of the game, one is ascribing to it properties over and above the possession of these markings. The predicate gets its meaning from the whole structure of the game. So with the language in which we ascribe P-predicates. To say that the criteria on the strength of which we ascribe P-predicates to others are of a logically adequate kind for this ascription, is not to say that all there is to the ascriptive meaning of those predicates is these criteria.

I am not at all sure what point Strawson is making here, but the following is suggested to me:

We are inclined to say that any card with the appropriate markings will be a Queen of Hearts, even that these markings determine, mean, that the card is the Queen of Hearts. But that it is the Queen of Hearts is, in large part, a matter of its having certain roles in various card games, and, of course, it is not a necessary or an analytic truth that a card with these markings has these roles in these games. So despite appearances it is not an analytic fact that a card with these markings is the Queen of Hearts. Nevertheless it is, in some sense, part of, a consequence of, the meaning of 'Queen of Hearts' that cards with these markings are called the Queen of Hearts. It is part of the meaning at least in the sense that to understand what is meant by 'Queen of Hearts' is, at least in part, to understand that that is the name for cards with these markings. If 'Queen of Hearts' were to become the name of some card with different markings this would involve at least some change in the meaning of 'Queen of Hearts'. The point seems to be that although it is not an analytic truth that a card with these markings is the Queen of Hearts, the meaning of 'Queen of Hearts', the criteria for being the Queen of Hearts, are such as to lay it down that if a card has these markings it is (what we call) the Queen of Hearts.

Much the same point might be made another way. Suppose there were a people who played exactly the same card games as we do, and with exactly the same cards, except that they used the Queen as we use the Jack, and vice versa. They might call the card with the Queen's markings 'The Queen of Hearts', but it is clear that 'Queen of Hearts' would not mean for them quite what it does for us. It is not an analytic or necessary truth that a card with these markings has such and such a role in various card games, yet it is, somehow, built into what *we* mean by 'Queen of Hearts' that a card with these markings has these roles. Thus our definition of 'Queen of Hearts' has an empirical element built into it; the use and meaning we give the term are founded on the fact that the card with these markings happens to be used in these ways.

In fact it is quite common for our terms and concepts to incorporate an empirical element in this way. Another example is the concept of solidity. The term 'solid' has built into it the empirical claim that things which block our

motion feel hard. We saw that it seems to be part of the
definition of 'Queen of Hearts' that a card with certain
markings is the Queen of Hearts, and also part of the definition that the Queen of Hearts has various roles in various
games, even though it is not an analytic or necessary fact that
a card with those markings has those roles in those games.
Similarly it seems to me part of the definition of 'solid'
that something which blocks our motion is solid, and also
part of the definition that solid things feel hard, even though
it is not an analytic or necessary fact that things which block
our motion feel hard. It is quite possible that things should
block our motion as solid things do without our being able
to feel them at all.

In some cases a concept, and hence the definition of the
relevant term, incorporates an empirical generalization which
is in fact false. 'The story of the man going round the squirrel
that always faces him shows that our concept of going round
includes the false idea that moving so as to be successively
at all directions from an object entails moving so as to see
successively all sides of that object.'[1] Similarly it might be said
that the term 'nigger' has built into its meaning the non-
analytic, and actually false, claim that black people are
despicable.

Strawson's claim was that 'the distinctive markings of a
certain card constitute a logically adequate criterion for calling it the Queen of Hearts'. Yet, as we have just seen, it does
not necessarily follow from the fact that it has those markings
that it is the Queen of Hearts, for a card might have those
markings and yet not be a Queen of Hearts because it has

[1] Robinson, *Definition* (Oxford), p. 182. Cf. also Malcolm on conflict
of criteria, *Dreaming*, p. 23.

none of the functions of a Queen of Hearts. What does necessarily follow from the fact that it has those markings is that it is *what we would call* a Queen of Hearts. That is, it would not be an abuse of the meaning of 'Queen of Hearts' to say of a card with the Queen's markings that it was not a Queen, where it was not used as one. But it would be an abuse of the meaning of 'Queen of Hearts' to say of a card with the Queen's markings that it was not what we would call a Queen of Hearts, even if it does turn out that it is not used as one. This is because the definition of 'Queen of Hearts' has built into it the fact that cards with these markings are used as Queens. If we discovered cases where such cards are not used as Queens we would have to alter the meaning, the definition, which we have given to 'Queen of Hearts'. There is nothing particularly surprising about this. Factual discoveries and changes in our beliefs and opinions can lead us, as in the case of simultaneity, to alter or modify or even, as in the case of nigger, completely reject various concepts. 'It is an improvement of a concept to substitute for it a similar concept including fewer false statements or demands that reality does not satisfy. Our early concept of downness demands absolute directions of space; since there are none such, it is an improvement to substitute for it the concept of downness as direction towards some given centre of gravity' (Robinson, *Definition*, p. 183).

I have argued all along that 'Beings who exhibit pain-behaviour are feeling pains' is not a necessary analytic truth, just as I would argue that 'Cards with these markings are used in such-and-such ways in card games' is not a necessary analytic truth. Nevertheless we have seen that although it is not an analytic truth, it is part of the meaning which we have given to 'Queen of Hearts' that a card with these markings is to be called the Queen of Hearts. Similarly it might be said that although it is not an analytic truth, it is part of the meaning which we have given to 'feeling a pain' that a being who exhibits pain-behaviour is to be described as feeling a pain. This may well be what Strawson means when he says that behaviour provides a 'logically adequate criterion' for the ascription of conscious states to others.

Now criteria of this sort are to be distinguished from the criteria discussed in Chapter VI, Section 2. It does not follow from the satisfaction of such a criterion that the person does feel a pain. Nor does it follow that to say that he feels a pain would involve a correct use of 'feels a pain', for someone might say that he feels a pain meaning to assert merely that he is groaning, and that would be an incorrect use of the expression. Rather, what follows from the satisfaction of this criterion is that we are *justified in saying* that he feels a pain. Personally I am reluctant to describe these factors which justify us in saying something as 'criteria' at all. The term 'criterion' covers too many different things already. I would prefer to speak of 'warranting-conditions',[1] or perhaps 'warranting-criteria'. Nevertheless this may be not only what Strawson means by 'logically adequate criteria for the ascription' of something, but also what Wittgenstein meant by a criterion, at least in the *Philosophical Investigations*. Rogers Albritton has argued that Wittgenstein's conception of criteria changed: in the *Blue Book* criteria are whatever it is that we refer to as, for example, having toothache; but in the *Philosophical Investigations* criteria are features such that 'anyone who is aware that the man is behaving in this manner, under these

[1] I owe this term to Mr. R. Ziedins, who owes it to Professor D. Gasking.

circumstances, is *justified in saying* that the man has a tooth-ache, in the absence of any special reason to say anything more guarded' (Albritton, 'On Wittgenstein's Use of the Term "Criterion" ', *Journal of Philosophy*, 1959, p. 856. His italics).

Thus I would want to say that pain-behaviour constitutes not a condition or a criterion of feeling a pain, but a warrant-ing-condition; and similarly that the markings constitute not a condition or a criterion of being the Queen of Hearts, but a warranting-condition. That is, the fact that a card has certain markings does not *mean* that it is the Queen of Hearts, for it might turn out not to be used as one. What it does mean is that we are justified, even if mistaken, in calling it a Queen of Hearts. It follows from the fact that it has these markings, together with the definition of 'Queen of Hearts', not that it is a Queen of Hearts, but that it is the sort of card we refer to as a Queen of Hearts. If, as is logically possible, it turns out not to be a Queen of Hearts, then so much the worse for our definition of 'Queen of Hearts'.

Similarly, the fact that a being behaves in a certain way does not *mean* that he feels a pain, but it does mean that we are justified, even if mistaken, in saying that he feels a pain. It follows from the fact that he behaves in this way, together with our definition of 'feeling a pain', not that he does feel a pain, but that this is the sort of situation which we describe as someone's feeling a pain. The point is that the meaning we give to 'feeling a pain', like the meaning we give to 'Queen of Hearts', incorporates and depends upon an empirical fact, the fact that people who exhibit pain-behaviour feel pains.

The conclusion is, then, that the meaning we give to 'feeling a pain', i.e. our concept of pain, itself spans the logical gap between pain sensation and pain-behaviour, in-asmuch as it contains and depends upon the claim that where there is pain-behaviour there is a pain sensation. The mean-ing we give to 'pain' itself guarantees our right to say of someone who exhibits the behaviour that he feels the sensa-tion. This conclusion fits with much of what Strawson wants to say, and it also fits with what a lot of other people have wanted to say about the absurdity of suggesting that be-haviour cannot entitle us to say that another feels a pain.

Personally I feel that this conclusion needs to be modified. For the fact is that people sometimes do exhibit the usual behavioural marks of feeling a pain, without actually feeling one. So our concept of pain does not guarantee that when-ever a person exhibits pain-behaviour it is correct to say that he feels a pain; it is possible to say that such a person does not feel a pain, without this being tantamount to a rejection of our concept of pain. Pain-behaviour is a criterion, in Straw-son's sense, for saying that someone feels a pain, but it is not a 'logically adequate', or at any rate not a 'logically sufficient', one. In order for it to follow, as a matter of necessity, that we are justified in saying of someone that he feels a pain, it is necessary not only that he display at least a tendency to pain-behaviour, but also that he is not acting in a play, acting under post-hypnotic suggestion, and so on. A logically sufficient justification for saying that he felt a pain would be a very complex, perhaps impossible, thing to state in its entirety.[1] So let us be content to say that pain-behaviour provides *a justification*, and a good one, for say-ing that someone feels a pain. It may be that Strawson is confused between saying that pain-behaviour is a logically

[1] Cf. Malcolm on p. 114 of *Knowledge and Certainty*.

sufficient justification for saying that someone feels a pain (which it is not); and saying that it is a matter of logic that pain-behaviour is a justification, though not a logically complete justification, for saying that someone feels a pain. That is, it may be that a person displays pain-behaviour without our being justified in saying that he feels a pain, because he is acting on a stage. But in so far as a person displays pain-behaviour it follows, as a matter of logic, or language, or 'grammar', that we are thus far justified in saying that he feels a pain.

To sum up: pain-behaviour constitutes a warranting-condition for the ascription of pain to others, in that our concept of pain, the meaning we give to 'feeling a pain', is such as to guarantee, to a considerable extent, the correctness of saying of someone who exhibits pain-behaviour that he feels a pain. Our concept of pain guarantees this, even though it is not a logical or analytic truth, because our concept of pain incorporates, is built upon, the contingent fact that pain-behaviour and pain sensation usually, characteristically, normally, go together. It is not a part or a consequence of the meaning of 'pain' that pain-behaviour entails feeling a pain, but it is a part of, a consequence of, the meaning we give to 'pain' that if a man exhibits pain-behaviour we have a strong justification for saying that he feels a pain.

2. The sceptic's next move should be obvious. He will say: What you have shown is that our concept of pain is founded upon, indeed incorporates, a certain fundamental belief about other people, the belief that when they exhibit pain-behaviour they are, other things being equal, feeling pains. But what I have been saying all along is that this belief cannot be proved

correct. So what you have shown is only that our concept of pain is founded upon, indeed incorporates, a belief which may well, for all you can show, be false. True, you have shown that I cannot both use this concept and say that the fact that people exhibit pain-behaviour does not show that they are feeling pains, any more than I can accept the concept of a nigger and deny that black people are despicable. If I want to say or even suggest that those who exhibit pain-behaviour might never be feeling pains, then I will have to reject or at least modify the accepted concept of pain, just as I would reject or modify the concept of nigger. But the fact remains that our use of the expression 'feels a pain' is based on a belief which may well, for all we can show, be false, and hence that our concept of pain may well, for all we can show, be to this extent misconceived. And this is a risk we should prefer not to run. If we cannot prove that people who exhibit pain-behaviour do feel pains, then it would be better if we modified our concept of pain in such a way that the behaviour did not provide a justification for saying that a pain is felt.

Now we might be prepared to accept this point. We might agree that our concept of pain is founded upon a belief which could be mistaken, and we might concede that the concept could be modified in the way that the sceptic suggests. Nevertheless it is with our existing concepts that we are concerned, and our existing concept is such as to justify our saying that the bleeding, groaning man feels a pain. Why should we alter our concepts just to please the sceptic? This is the sort of attitude most of us take to the sceptic about all empirical knowledge, the man who says that we cannot know any matter of fact because any matter of fact might be otherwise. We say: if you alter the concept of knowledge so that only what cannot be otherwise, only what is logically necessary, can be known, then of course we cannot know any matter of fact. But this is not the concept of knowledge we actually do use, and we see no reason for accepting, indeed good reason for rejecting, your modification of the concept. Similarly with the other minds sceptic: if we alter our concept of pain to suit him it follows that pain-behaviour no longer justifies our saying that a man feels pain. But why should we alter the concept in this way?

Notice that this is, in effect, to concede the sceptic's point. It is to agree that what he says is true enough, without agreeing that we ought therefore to do as he does—it is like agreeing that jazz is a valid art form without becoming a jazz enthusiast yourself. But there is another, more extreme, reply to the sceptic. We might argue that we cannot change our concept of pain in the way suggested, that a concept, any concept, of pain is possible only in so far as it incorporates this belief that behaviour and sensation characteristically go together. To say this is not to concede the sceptic's point; it is to say that he is attempting the logically impossible. For if it is impossible to have or use a concept of pain unless it incorporates some such belief as that when people exhibit pain-behaviour they are feeling pains, then it is impossible to modify our talk about pains in the way that the sceptic suggests.

For my own part, I take the stronger line. As Wittgenstein said, 'An "inner process" stands in need of outward criteria'. There must be something, some publicly observable phenomenon, which entitles us to say of someone that he feels a pain, or any other sensation. This is because there must be some way of explaining, teaching, and checking the use, the meaning, of the expression 'feels a pain'. If this expression is to be genuinely meaningful, there must be something which counts as feeling a pain, and it must be possible to establish, publicly, what this something is. This does not mean that there must be public criteria which establish that a certain person does feel a pain, any more than there must be public criteria which establish that someone is a witch (cf. pp. 118–19 above). The point is only that there must be public criteria which establish what counts as feeling a pain, being a witch. We explain what is meant by 'feeling a pain' by reference to observable phenomena such as behaviour, just as we explain what is meant by 'witch' by reference to observable phenomena such as reciting spells and flying on broomsticks. It does not follow from the behaviour that the person feels a pain any more than it follows from reciting spells, or even from flying on a broomstick, that the person is in league with the devil. But it does follow from the way we teach and explain 'feels a pain' that the person's behaviour is a reason for saying that he feels a pain. Indeed, if there is to be any way at all of teaching and explaining 'feels a pain', then there must be some publicly observable phenomena which provide some justification for saying that someone feels a pain.

This is the basic truth that underlies the three arguments we considered: the private language argument, the argument from criteria, the argument from persons. Put most simply the point is that if a term or expression is to be genuinely meaningful it must be possible to explain, to others, what it means, how it is used, etc. So there must be public phenomena by reference to which we can teach and learn the meaning of that term or expression. In the case of 'feels a pain' it is obvious that the phenomena in question are going to be the way the person behaves, since it is this that establishes that what is felt is a pain. If 'feels a pain' is and must be taught by reference to such things as bleeding and groaning, then bleeding and groaning must as a matter of logic, of language, of 'grammar', provide reasons for saying that someone feels a pain. So if, like the sceptic, we refuse to accept bleeding and groaning as justifying us in saying that someone feels a pain, we make it impossible to talk about feeling pains at all. Or more generally, unless we accepted something as providing a justification, a criterion in Strawson's sense, for the ascription of conscious states to others, we would be unable to speak about conscious states at all.

The three arguments characteristically try to make too much of this point. For it does not show that what the sceptic says is false, much less that it is incoherent, cannot be said—so long as the sceptic's claim is only that our ascription of pains and the like to others is based on a belief which might, for all we can show, be false. It shows only that pain-behaviour, or something of the sort, must justify us in saying that another feels a pain; it does not show that pain-behaviour must establish that another does feel a pain. The sceptic can still insist that we could be mistaken in our belief that when others exhibit pain-behaviour they are feeling pains; what he cannot do is insist that this belief actually is mistaken, and yet continue to speak about pains. Now the sceptic does not want to say that the belief actually is false. Typically the philosophical sceptic holds not that what we claim to know is false, but that we cannot know whether it is true or false—his argument is that, true or false, we are not in a position to claim *knowledge*.

My own reply to the sceptic (p. 68 above) was that the fact that we cannot prove the truth of this belief does

not show that we do not know. The way we talk about
knowledge and about other minds establishes that—given
the truth of what we claim to know, and this is not what the
sceptic is questioning—we do have knowledge of other
minds, and nothing that the sceptic does or could say can
prove otherwise. Nevertheless what the sceptic says does
seem to show that what we accept as knowledge of other
minds is, in a way, 'inferior' to other types of knowledge,
and therefore that it would perhaps be preferable if we did
not accept it as knowledge in the way that we do. But I said
we need not be worried about the status of our knowledge
of other minds so long as we can show that this belief, 'the
other minds belief', on which the knowledge is founded, is
justified. We saw that, in any practical sense, we obviously
are justified in believing that when other people bleed and
groan they are feeling pains. The question was whether we
could provide a theoretical justification for our accepting the
belief as true. This has now been done. The belief is justified,
theoretically as well as practically, inasmuch as we have to
accept it as true if we are to talk about conscious states, even
our own, at all.

   This seems to me to be the correct answer to scepticism
about our knowledge of other minds. We have knowledge
of other minds in so far as our 'belief in other minds' is
correct. Perhaps this belief is mistaken. Perhaps we cannot
prove that it is correct. Perhaps we do not have knowledge
of other minds after all. But we have to accept the belief as
correct, we have to accept what people say and do as evidence
for what goes on in their minds, if we are to speak about
other minds in the first place.

Index